Mmmm...
Mmmm...
Mmmm...
Mmmm...
Mmmm...
Mmmm...
Mmmm...
Mmmm...
Mmmm...

Mmmm...
Pasta

Mmmm...
Pasta

First edition published in 2010
LOVE FOOD is an imprint of Parragon Books Ltd

Parragon
Queen Street House
4 Queen Street
Bath BA1 1HE, UK

ISBN: 978-1-4075-9088-2

Printed in China

Design by Talking Design
Cover photography by Charlie Richards
Cover image styled by Mary Wall
Introduction by Linda Doeser

Notes for the Reader
This book uses imperial, metric, and US cup measurements. Follow the same units of measurement throughout; do not mix imperial and metric. All spoon measurements are level: teaspoons are assumed to be 5 ml, and tablespoons are assumed to be 15 ml. Unless otherwise stated, milk is assumed to be whole, eggs and individual vegetables, such as potatoes, are medium, and pepper is freshly ground black pepper.

The times given are an approximate guide only. Preparation times differ according to the techniques used by different people and the cooking times may also vary from those given as a result of the type of oven used. Optional ingredients, variations, or serving suggestions have not been included in the calculations.

Recipes using raw or very lightly cooked eggs should be avoided by infants, the elderly, pregnant women, convalescents, and anyone with a chronic condition. Pregnant and breast-feeding women are advised to avoid eating peanuts and peanut products. People with nut allergies should be aware that some of the prepared ingredients used in the recipes in this book may contain nuts. Always check the packaging before use.

Vegetarians should be aware that some of the ready-prepared ingredients used in the recipes in this book may contain animal products. Always check the packaging before use.

contents

introduction

It's no wonder that pasta is one of the world's most popular foods—it's easy to cook, inexpensive, nutritious, a convenient pantry ingredient, and, above all, the basis for an abundance of wonderfully delicious dishes. It goes with almost every other ingredient imaginable—fish and shellfish, meat and poultry, vegetables, mushrooms, cheese, eggs, cream, nuts, herbs, spices, and even fruit. This astonishing versatility makes it the perfect choice for every occasion, whether you want a quick and easy midweek supper dish for the family or an elegant appetizer for a special occasion.

types of pasta

There are over 200 pasta shapes with three times as many names, so knowing which type to use can seem a little daunting. An easy rule of thumb is to choose thick pasta strands, such as tagliatelle, papardelle, and tagliarini, for thick creamy sauces, long thin strands, such as spaghetti, vermicelli, and bucatini, for shellfish sauces, and tubular pasta, such as rigatoni, penne, and pipe, to trap chunky rustic sauces. Each recipe in this book suggests a suitable type of pasta, but you can easily substitute your favorite shape or just use whatever you have at hand. Children particularly like the more interesting shapes, such as fusilli (pasta spirals), conchiglie (pasta shells), farfalle (pasta bows), and orecchiette (ear-shaped pasta), and these are also ideal for pasta salads. Filled and baked pasta dishes are most commonly made with lasagna sheets, cannelloni tubes, macaroni, and various little "parcels" that may be square, round, half moons, or folded. Pasta for soups is very tiny and comes in all kinds of fancy shapes, such as stars, serrated rings, and "melon seeds."

Pasta may be dried or fresh. When buying dried pasta, check the package to make sure that it has been made from durum wheat flour. This is a hard wheat with a high gluten content that is also ground into semolina, a term that may be used to describe pasta flour. Dried pasta made totally or partly from most other flours may be cheaper but will become sticky during cooking. Dried pasta is a creamy color, while fresh egg pasta is golden yellow.

Fresh and dried pasta may also be flavored and colored. Orange-red (tomato) pasta and green (spinach) pasta are the best-known types. Their flavor is mild and they are often served

together or with plain pasta. Beet produces a spectacularly vibrant color with a delicate flavor, while porcini turn the pasta dough golden brown and give it a full earthy flavor. Squid ink is a traditional flavoring ingredient, which produces dramatic-looking black pasta that is perfect with shellfish sauces. Herbs and spices are also used to flavor fresh pasta.

Most supermarkets stock packages of filled and unfilled fresh pasta in the refrigerated section, although not all shapes are available. A larger selection of filled pasta, often made on the premises, will be found in Italian delicatessens. Fresh pasta cooks more quickly than dried but must be eaten within a few days of purchase. Making your own fresh pasta is not difficult and although time-consuming, is very satisfying. You don't have to buy expensive equipment; the tools you use for making pastry dough are adequate. However, if making ravioli, agnolotti, and tortellini becomes an absorbing pastime, you might consider investing in a pasta machine, which makes rolling out the dough quicker and easier, pasta cutting wheels, a ravioli cutter, and a ravioli tray.

cooking pasta

It is important that the pasta has plenty of room to swell and move freely, so always use a large pan. Otherwise, as the starch is released, the pasta becomes sticky. Some cooks recommend adding a tablespoon of olive oil to the cooking water to prevent this, but others disagree. You'll have to make up your own mind. Salt, on the other hand, is absolutely essential. Those worried about too much salt in the modern diet should note that it is very diluted and little is absorbed by the pasta itself. Allow 4¼ quarts/4 liters water and 3 tablespoons salt for every 1 lb/450 g pasta (fresh or dried).

Bring the salted water to a brisk boil. If using small pasta shapes, sprinkle them in immediately and bring back to a boil. If using strands, gradually ease them into the water so that they soften and bend and then bring back to a boil. Start timing the cooking from the moment that water returns to a boil, continuing to boil briskly rather than simmering. The cooking time depends on a number of factors—whether the pasta is fresh or dried, filled or unfilled, its shape, the hardness of the water, and exactly how soft you consider al dente to be. Al dente, literally "to the tooth," means tender but still firm to the bite. The best way to test for "doneness" is to remove a small piece of pasta from the pan and bite it between your front teeth.

A guideline for cooking times is as follows but it is always sensible to start checking the pasta before the recommended time is up.

- Fresh unfilled pasta—2–3 minutes, less for very fine pasta.
- Fresh filled pasta—8–10 minutes.
- Dried unfilled pasta—8–12 minutes.
- Dried filled pasta—15–20 minutes.

When the pasta is al dente, drain it in a colander or remove from the pan with a spaghetti fork. It is not essential to drain off all traces of water. When serving hot, it should immediately be tossed or stirred with the sauce. If serving in a salad, drain and rinse in cold water, then stir with a little olive oil to prevent it from becoming sticky as it cools.

Traditional dried pasta for baking, such as lasagna sheets, requires precooking in boiling water—check the packet instructions. Fresh lasagna also needs precooking for about 2 minutes. Add it to the boiling water and remove it as soon as it rises to the surface. In both cases, drain, refresh in cold water, drain again, and spread out on clean dish towels. Modern dried lasagna and cannelloni may be layered or filled without precooking—again, check the packet instructions.

béchamel sauce

Makes 1¼ cups

- 1¼ cups milk
- 1 bay leaf
- 6 black peppercorns
- slice of onion
- mace blade
- 2 tbsp butter
- ¼ cup all-purpose flour
- salt and pepper

1 Pour the milk into a saucepan and add the bay leaf, peppercorns, onion, and mace. Bring to just below boiling point, then remove the saucepan from the heat, cover, and let steep for 10 minutes. Strain the milk into a pitcher and discard the flavorings.

2 Melt the butter in another saucepan. Add the flour and cook over low heat, stirring constantly, for 2 minutes. Remove the saucepan from the heat and gradually stir in the flavored milk.

3 Return the saucepan to low heat and bring to a boil, stirring constantly. Cook, stirring constantly, until thickened and smooth. Season with salt and pepper.

basic pasta dough

Serves 3-4

- 1¾ cups white bread flour, plus extra for dusting
- pinch of salt
- 2 eggs, lightly beaten
- 1 tbsp olive oil

1 Sift together the flour and salt onto a counter and make a well in the center with your fingers. Pour the eggs and oil into the well, then using the fingers of one hand, gradually incorporate the flour into the liquid.

2 Knead the dough on a lightly floured counter until it is completely smooth. Wrap in plastic wrap and let rest for 30 minutes before rolling out or feeding through a pasta machine. Resting makes the dough more elastic.

flavored pasta

Basic pasta dough may be flavored and colored by the addition of other ingredients.

Tomato pasta: Add 2 tablespoons tomato paste to the well in the flour and use only 1½ eggs instead of 2.

Spinach pasta: Blanch 8 oz/225 g spinach in boiling water for 1 minute, then drain, and squeeze out as much as possible. Alternatively, use 5½ oz/150 g thawed frozen spinach. This does not need blanching, but as much liquid as possible should be squeezed out. Finely chop the spinach and mix with the flour before making a well and adding the eggs and oil.

Herb pasta: Add 3 tablespoons finely chopped fresh herbs to the flour before making a well and adding the eggs and oil.

Saffron pasta: Soak an envelope of powdered saffron in 2 tablespoons of hot water for 15 minutes. Use 1½ eggs and whisk the saffron water into them.

Whole wheat pasta: Use 1¼ cups whole wheat flour with ¼ cup white bread flour.

Mmmm...
soups & salads

fresh tomato soup

serves 4

- 1 tbsp olive oil
- 1 lb 7 oz/650 g plum tomatoes
- 1 onion, cut into quarters
- 1 garlic clove, thinly sliced
- 1 celery stalk, coarsely chopped
- 2 cups chicken stock
- 2 oz/55 g dried macaroni
- salt and pepper
- chopped fresh flat-leaf parsley, to garnish

1 Heat the oil in a large saucepan and add the tomatoes, onion, garlic, and celery. Cover and cook over low heat for 45 minutes, occasionally shaking the saucepan gently, until the mixture is pulpy.

2 Transfer the mixture to a food processor or blender and process to a smooth puree. Push the puree through a strainer into a clean pan.

3 Add the stock and bring to a boil. Add the pasta, return to a boil, and cook for 8–10 minutes, until the pasta is tender but still firm to the bite. Season to taste with salt and pepper. Ladle into warmed bowls, sprinkle with the parsley, and serve.

minestrone soup

serves 4

- 1 tbsp. olive oil
- 1 onion, finely chopped
- 1 large carrot, diced
- 2 celery stalks, trimmed and sliced
- 1 bouquet garni
- 14 oz/400 g canned chopped tomatoes
- 2 oz/55 g dried soup pasta shells or spaghetti broken into short lengths
- 3½ cups vegetable stock
- ½ small cabbage, about 8 oz/225 g
- pepper

1 Heat the oil in a large saucepan, add the onion, carrot, and celery and cook gently for 5 minutes, stirring frequently. Add the bouquet garni with the tomatoes. Fill the empty tomato can halfway with water, swirl to remove all the remaining tomatoes, then pour into the saucepan.

2 Add the pasta with the stock and bring to a boil. Reduce the heat to a simmer and cook for 12 minutes, or until the vegetables are almost tender.

3 Discard any outer leaves and hard central core from the cabbage and shred. Wash well, then add to the pan with pepper to taste. Continue to cook for 5–8 minutes, or until all the vegetables are tender, but still firm to the bite. Ladle into warmed bowls and serve.

brown lentil & pasta soup

serves 4

- 4 strips lean bacon, cut into small squares
- 1 onion, chopped
- 2 garlic cloves, crushed
- 2 celery stalks, chopped
- 1¾ oz/50 g dried farfallini (small pasta bows)
- 14 oz/400 g canned brown lentils, drained
- 5 cups vegetable stock
- 2 tbsp chopped fresh mint, plus extra sprigs to garnish

1 Place the bacon in a large skillet together with the onion, garlic, and celery. Cook for 4–5 minutes, stirring, until the onion is tender and the bacon is just beginning to brown.

2 Add the pasta to the skillet and cook, stirring, for 1 minute, to coat the pasta in the fat.

3 Add the lentils and the stock and bring to a boil. Reduce the heat and simmer for 12–15 minutes, or until the pasta is tender but still firm to the bite.

4 Remove the skillet from the heat and stir in the chopped fresh mint. Ladle into warmed bowls, garnish with fresh mint sprigs, and serve.

bean & pasta soup

serves 4

- 1⅓ cups dried navy beans, soaked, drained, and rinsed
- 4 tbsp olive oil
- 2 large onions, sliced
- 3 garlic cloves, chopped
- 14 oz/400 g canned chopped tomatoes
- 1 tsp dried oregano
- 1 tsp tomato paste
- 3 cups water
- 3 oz/85 g dried macaroni
- 1 cup thinly sliced, drained sun-dried tomatoes
- 1 tbsp chopped fresh cilantro or flat-leaf parsley
- salt and pepper
- freshly grated Parmesan cheese, to serve

1 Put the beans into a saucepan, cover with water, and bring to a boil. Boil rapidly for 10 minutes to remove any toxins, then drain and rinse.

2 Heat the oil in a large saucepan over medium heat. Add the onions and cook until they are just starting to change color. Stir in the garlic and cook for an additional minute. Stir in the chopped tomatoes, oregano, and the tomato paste and pour over the water.

3 Add the cooked, drained beans to the mixture in the saucepan, bring to a boil and cover. Simmer for about 45 minutes, or until the beans are almost tender.

4 Add the pasta, season to taste with salt and pepper, and stir in the sun-dried tomatoes. Return the soup to a boil, partially cover, and continue cooking for 10 minutes, or until the pasta is tender but still firm to the bite.

5 Stir in the chopped cilantro. Taste the soup and adjust the seasoning, if necessary. Ladle the soup into warmed bowls, sprinkle with the Parmesan, and serve.

potato & pesto soup

serves 4

- 2 tbsp olive oil
- 3 strips smoked bacon, chopped
- 2 tbsp butter
- 1 lb/450 g starchy potatoes, finely chopped
- 1 lb/450 g onions, finely chopped
- 2½ cups chicken stock
- 2½ cups milk
- 3½ oz/100 g dried conchigliette (small pasta shells)
- ⅔ cup heavy cream
- 2 tbsp chopped fresh flat-leaf parsley
- 2 tbsp fresh or store-bought pesto
- salt and pepper
- freshly grated Parmesan cheese, to serve

1 Heat the oil in a large saucepan and cook the bacon over medium heat for 4 minutes. Add the butter, potatoes, and onions, and cook for 12 minutes, stirring constantly.

2 Add the stock and milk to the saucepan, bring to a boil, and simmer for 5 minutes. Add the conchigliette and simmer for an additional 3–5 minutes.

3 Blend in the cream and simmer for 5 minutes. Add the chopped parsley, pesto, and salt and pepper to taste. Ladle into warmed bowls and serve with the Parmesan.

tuscan veal broth

serves 4

- ⅓ cup dried peas, soaked for 2 hours and drained
- 2 lb/900 g boned neck of veal, diced
- 5 cups beef stock
- 2½ cups water
- ⅓ cup pearl barley, washed
- 1 large carrot, diced
- 1 small turnip, about 6 oz/175 g, diced
- 1 large leek, thinly sliced
- 1 red onion, finely chopped
- ½ cup chopped tomatoes
- 1 fresh basil sprig
- 3½ oz/100 g dried vermicelli (thin pasta strands)
- salt and pepper

1 Put the peas, veal, stock, and water into a large saucepan and bring to a boil over low heat. Using a slotted spoon, skim off any foam that rises to the surface.

2 When all of the foam has been removed, add the pearl barley and a pinch of salt to the mixture. Simmer gently over low heat for 25 minutes.

3 Add the carrot, turnip, leek, onion, tomatoes, and basil to the saucepan, and season to taste with salt and pepper. Simmer for about 2 hours, skimming the surface from time to time to remove any foam. Remove the saucepan from the heat and set aside for 2 hours.

4 Set the pan over medium heat and bring to a boil. Add the vermicelli and cook for 4–5 minutes, or until the pasta is tender but still firm to the bite. Season to taste with salt and pepper, then remove and discard the basil. Ladle into warmed serving bowls and serve.

chicken & chickpea soup

serves 4

- 2 tbsp butter
- 3 scallions, chopped
- 2 garlic cloves, finely chopped
- 1 fresh marjoram sprig, finely chopped
- 12 oz/350 g skinless, boneless chicken breasts, diced
- 5 cups chicken stock
- 12 oz/350 g canned chickpeas, drained and rinsed
- 1 bouquet garni
- 1 red bell pepper, diced
- 1 green bell pepper, diced
- 4 oz/115 g dried macaroni
- salt and pepper
- croutons, to serve

1 Melt the butter in a large saucepan over medium heat. Add the scallions, garlic, marjoram, and chicken and cook, stirring frequently, for 5 minutes.

2 Add the stock, chickpeas, and bouquet garni, then season to taste with salt and pepper.

3 Bring the soup to a boil over medium heat, then reduce the heat and simmer for about 2 hours.

4 Add the diced bell peppers and pasta to the saucepan, then simmer for an additional 20 minutes.

5 Ladle into warmed serving bowls, sprinkle over the croutons, and serve.

italian chicken soup

serves 4

- 1 lb/450 g skinless, boneless chicken breast, cut into thin strips
- 5 cups chicken stock
- ⅔ cup heavy cream
- 4 oz/115 g dried vermicelli (thin pasta strands)
- 1 tbsp cornstarch
- 3 tbsp milk
- 6 oz/175 g canned corn kernels, drained
- salt and pepper

1 Place the chicken in a large saucepan and pour in the chicken stock and cream. Bring to a boil, then reduce the heat and simmer for 20 minutes.

2 Meanwhile, bring a large saucepan of lightly salted water to a boil. Add the pasta, return to a boil, and cook for 8–10 minutes, or until tender but still firm to the bite. Drain the pasta well and keep warm.

3 Season the soup to taste with salt and pepper. Mix the cornstarch and milk together until a smooth paste forms, then stir it into the soup. Add the corn and pasta and heat through. Ladle the soup into warmed bowls, add extra seasoning if liked, and serve.

fish soup with macaroni

serves 6

- 2 tbsp olive oil
- 2 onions, sliced
- 1 garlic clove, finely chopped
- 4 cups fish stock or water
- 14 oz/400 g canned chopped tomatoes
- 1/4 tsp herbes de Provence
- 1/4 tsp saffron threads
- 4 oz/115 g dried macaroni
- 18 mussels, scrubbed and debearded
- 1 lb/450 g monkfish fillet, cut into chunks
- 8 oz/225 g shrimp, shelled and deveined, tails left on
- salt and pepper

1 Heat the oil in a large saucepan. Add the onions and garlic and cook over low heat, stirring occasionally, for 5 minutes, or until the onions have softened.

2 Add the stock with the tomatoes and their can juices, herbs, saffron, and pasta, and season to taste with salt and pepper. Bring to a boil, then cover and simmer for 15 minutes.

3 Discard any mussels with broken shells or any that refuse to close when tapped. Add the mussels, monkfish, and shrimp to the saucepan. Re-cover and simmer for an additional 5–10 minutes, until the mussels have opened, the shrimp have changed color, and the fish is opaque and flakes easily. Discard any mussels that remain closed. Ladle the soup into warmed bowls and serve.

mussel & pasta soup

serves 4

- 1 lb 10 oz/750 g mussels, scrubbed and debearded
- 2 tbsp olive oil
- ½ cup butter
- 2 oz/55 g rindless lean bacon, chopped
- 1 onion, chopped
- 2 garlic cloves, finely chopped
- scant ½ cup all-purpose flour
- 3 potatoes, thinly sliced
- 4 oz/115 g dried farfalle (pasta bows)
- 1¼ cups heavy cream
- 1 tbsp lemon juice
- 2 egg yolks
- salt and pepper
- finely chopped fresh flat-leaf parsley, to garnish

1 Discard any mussels with broken shells or any that refuse to close when tapped. Bring a large, heavy-bottom saucepan of water to a boil. Add the mussels and oil and season to taste with pepper. Cover tightly and cook over high heat for 5 minutes, or until the mussels have opened. Remove the mussels with a slotted spoon, discarding any that remain closed. Strain the cooking liquid and set aside 5 cups.

2 Melt the butter in a clean pan. Add the bacon, onion, and garlic, and cook over low heat, stirring occasionally, for 5 minutes. Stir in the flour and cook, stirring, for 1 minute. Gradually stir in all but 2 tablespoons of the reserved cooking liquid and bring to a boil, stirring constantly. Add the potato slices and simmer for 5 minutes. Add the pasta and simmer for an additional 10 minutes.

3 Stir in the cream and lemon juice and season to taste with salt and pepper. Add the mussels. Mix the egg yolks and the remaining mussel cooking liquid together, then stir the mixture into the soup and cook for 4 minutes, until thickened.

4 Ladle the soup into warmed serving bowls, garnish with the chopped parsley, and serve.

italian salad

serves 4

- 8 oz/225 g dried conchiglie (pasta shells)
- ⅓ cup pine nuts
- 2¼ cups halved cherry tomatoes
- 1 red bell pepper, seeded and cut into bite-size chunks
- 1 red onion, chopped
- 7 oz/200 g buffalo mozzarella, cubed
- 12 black olives, pitted
- 1 cup fresh basil leaves
- shavings of fresh Parmesan cheese and crusty bread, to serve
- salt and pepper

dressing

- 5 tbsp extra virgin olive oil
- 2 tbsp balsamic vinegar
- 1 tbsp chopped fresh basil

1 Bring a large saucepan of lightly salted water to a boil. Add the pasta, return to a boil, and cook over medium heat for 8–10 minutes, or until tender but still firm to the bite. Drain, rinse under cold running water, and drain again. Let cool.

2 Put the pine nuts in a dry skillet and cook over low heat for 1–2 minutes, until golden brown. Remove from the heat, transfer to a dish, and let cool.

3 To make the dressing, put the oil, vinegar, and basil into a small bowl. Season with salt and pepper to taste and stir together well. Cover with plastic wrap and set to one side.

4 To assemble the salad, place the pasta in a serving bowl. Add the pine nuts, tomatoes, red bell pepper, onion, cheese, and olives. Scatter over the basil leaves, then drizzle over the dressing. Serve with the Parmesan and crusty bread.

pear & bleu cheese salad

serves 4

- 9 oz/250 g dried orecchiette (ear-shaped pasta)
- 1 head radicchio, torn into pieces
- 1 oak leaf lettuce, torn into pieces
- 2 pears, halved, cored, and diced
- 1 tbsp lemon juice
- 9 oz/250 g bleu cheese, diced
- scant ½ cup chopped walnuts
- 4 tomatoes, quartered
- 1 red onion, sliced
- 1 carrot, grated
- 8 fresh basil leaves
- ⅓ cup corn kernels
- salt and pepper

dressing

- 2 tbsp lemon juice
- 4 tbsp olive oil
- 4 tbsp balsamic vinegar

1 Bring a large saucepan of lightly salted water to a boil. Add the pasta, return to a boil, and cook for 8–10 minutes, or until tender but still firm to the bite. Drain, refresh in a bowl of cold water, and drain again.

2 For the dressing, mix the lemon juice, olive oil, and vinegar together in a pitcher, then season to taste with salt and pepper.

3 Place the radicchio and oak leaf lettuce leaves in a large bowl. Halve the pears, remove the cores, and dice the flesh. Toss the diced pear with the lemon juice in a small bowl to prevent discoloration. Top the salad with the bleu cheese, walnuts, pears, tomatoes, onion slices, and grated carrot. Add the basil and corn kernels, pour over the dressing, and serve with extra pepper.

pasta salad with pesto vinaigrette

serves 6

- 8 oz/225 g dried fusilli (pasta spirals)
- 4 tomatoes, peeled
- ½ cup black olives
- 2 tbsp sun-dried tomatoes in oil, drained
- 2 tbsp pine nuts, dry-roasted
- 2 tbsp freshly grated Parmesan cheese
- salt and pepper
- fresh basil sprig, to garnish

pesto vinaigrette

- 4 tbsp chopped fresh basil
- 1 garlic clove, finely chopped
- 2 tbsp freshly grated Parmesan cheese
- 4 tbsp olive oil
- 2 tbsp lemon juice

1 Bring a large saucepan of lightly salted water to a boil over medium heat. Add the pasta, return to a boil, and cook for 8–10 minutes, or until tender but still firm to the bite. Drain the pasta thoroughly, rinse well in hot water, then drain again.

2 To make the pesto vinaigrette, whisk the basil, garlic, cheese, oil, and lemon juice together in a small bowl until well blended. Season to taste with pepper.

3 Put the pasta into a bowl, pour over the pesto vinaigrette, and toss thoroughly.

4 Cut the tomatoes into wedges. Halve and pit the olives, and slice the sun-dried tomatoes. Add the tomatoes, olives, and sun-dried tomatoes to the pasta and toss well.

5 Transfer the pasta to a serving bowl and sprinkle the pine nuts and Parmesan over the top. Garnish with a basil sprig and serve warm.

warm pasta salad

serves 4

- 8 oz/225 g dried farfalle (pasta bows)
- 6 pieces of sun-dried tomato in oil, drained and chopped
- 4 scallions, chopped
- 1¼ cups arugula, shredded
- ½ cucumber, seeded and diced
- salt and pepper

dressing

- 4 tbsp olive oil
- 1 tbsp white wine vinegar
- ½ tsp superfine sugar
- 1 tsp Dijon mustard
- 4 fresh basil leaves, finely shredded

1 To make the dressing, whisk the olive oil, vinegar, sugar, and mustard together in a pitcher. Season to taste with salt and pepper and stir in the basil.

2 Bring a large saucepan of lightly salted water to a boil. Add the pasta, return to a boil, and cook for 8–10 minutes, or until tender but still firm to the bite. Drain and transfer to a serving bowl. Add the dressing and toss well.

3 Add the tomatoes, scallions, arugula, and cucumber, season to taste with salt and pepper, and toss. Serve warm.

pasta salad with charbroiled bell peppers

serves 4

- 1 red bell pepper
- 1 orange bell pepper
- 10 oz/280 g dried conchiglie (pasta shells)
- 3 tbsp shredded fresh basil leaves
- salt and pepper

dressing

- 5 tbsp extra virgin olive oil
- 2 tbsp lemon juice
- 2 tbsp fresh or store-bought pesto
- 1 garlic clove, crushed

1 Put the whole bell peppers on a baking sheet and place under a preheated broiler, turning frequently, for 15 minutes, until charred all over. Remove with tongs and place in a bowl. Cover with crumpled paper towels and set aside.

2 Meanwhile, bring a large saucepan of lightly salted water to a boil. Add the pasta, return to a boil, and cook for 8–10 minutes, or until tender but still firm to the bite.

3 To make the dressing, combine the olive oil, lemon juice, pesto, and garlic in a serving bowl, whisking well to mix. Drain the pasta, add it to the pesto mixture while still hot, and toss well. Set aside.

4 When the bell peppers are cool enough to handle, peel off the skins, then cut open and remove the seeds. Chop the flesh coarsely and add to the pasta with the basil. Season to taste with salt and pepper and toss well. Serve warm.

roast beef salad

serves 4

- 1 lb 10 oz/750 g beef fillet, trimmed of any visible fat
- 2 tsp Worcestershire sauce
- 3 tbsp olive oil
- 14 oz/400 g green beans
- 3½ oz/100g dried orecchiette (ear-shaped pasta)
- 2 red onions, finely sliced
- 1 large head radicchio
- generous ¼ cup green olives, pitted
- scant ⅓ cup shelled hazelnuts, whole
- pepper

dressing

- 1 tsp Dijon mustard
- 2 tbsp white wine vinegar
- 5 tbsp olive oil

1 Preheat the oven to 425°F/220°C. Rub the beef with pepper to taste and Worcestershire sauce. Heat 2 tablespoons of the oil in a small roasting pan over high heat, add the beef, and sear on all sides. Transfer the dish to the preheated oven and roast for 30 minutes. Remove and let cool.

2 Bring a large saucepan of water to a boil, add the beans, and cook for 5 minutes, or until just tender. Remove with a slotted spoon and refresh the beans under cold running water. Drain and put into a large bowl.

3 Return the bean cooking water to a boil, add the pasta, and cook for 8–10 minutes, or until tender but still firm to the bite. Drain, return to the pan, and toss with the remaining oil.

4 Add the pasta to the beans with the onions, radicchio leaves, olives, and hazelnuts, mix gently and transfer to a serving bowl. Thinly slice the beef, then arrange some of the slices on top of the salad.

5 Whisk together the dressing ingredients in a separate bowl, then pour over the salad and serve at once with extra sliced beef.

spicy sausage salad

serves 4

- 4½ oz/125 g dried conchiglie (pasta shells)
- 2 tbsp olive oil
- 1 medium onion, chopped
- 2 garlic cloves, very finely chopped
- 1 small yellow bell pepper, seeded and cut into very thin sticks
- 6 oz/175 g spicy pork sausage, sliced
- 2 tbsp red wine
- 1 tbsp red wine vinegar
- 4 cups mixed salad greens
- salt

1 Bring a large saucepan of lightly salted water to a boil. Add the pasta, return to a boil, and cook for 8–10 minutes, or until tender but still firm to the bite.

2 Heat the oil in a saucepan over medium heat. Add the onion and cook until translucent, then stir in the garlic, yellow bell pepper, and sausage, and cook for 3–4 minutes, stirring once or twice.

3 Add the wine, wine vinegar, and reserved pasta to the pan, stir, and bring the mixture just to a boil over medium heat. Drain.

4 Place the salad greens in a serving bowl, spoon over the warm sausage-and-pasta mixture, and serve.

pasta salad with melon & shrimp

serves 6

- 8 oz/225 g dried green fusilli (pasta spirals)
- 5 tbsp extra virgin olive oil
- 1 lb/450 g cooked shrimp, peeled and deveined
- 1 cantaloupe melon
- 1 honeydew melon
- 1 tbsp red wine vinegar
- 1 tsp Dijon mustard
- pinch of superfine sugar
- 1 tbsp chopped fresh flat-leaf parsley
- 1 tbsp chopped fresh basil, plus extra leaves to garnish
- 1 oak leaf lettuce, shredded
- salt and pepper

1 Bring a large saucepan of lightly salted water to a boil. Add the pasta, return to a boil, and cook for 8–10 minutes, or until tender but still firm to the bite. Drain, toss with 1 tablespoon of the olive oil, and let cool.

2 Meanwhile, peel and devein the shrimp, then place them in a large bowl. Halve both the melons and scoop out the seeds with a spoon. Using a melon baller or teaspoon, scoop out balls of the flesh and add them to the shrimp.

3 Whisk together the remaining olive oil, the vinegar, mustard, sugar, parsley, and basil in a small bowl. Season to taste with salt and pepper. Add the cooled pasta to the shrimp-and-melon mixture and toss lightly to mix, then pour in the dressing, and toss again. Cover with plastic wrap and chill in the refrigerator for 30 minutes.

4 Place the shredded lettuce leaves in a serving bowl. Spoon the pasta salad on top, garnish with basil leaves, and serve.

pasta niçoise

serves 4

- 1 cup green beans, cut into 2-inch/5-cm lengths
- 8 oz/225 g dried fusilli (pasta spirals)
- generous ⅓ cup olive oil
- 2 tuna steaks, about 12 oz/350 g each
- 6 cherry tomatoes, halved
- ⅓ cup black olives, pitted and halved
- 6 canned anchovies, drained and chopped
- 3 tbsp chopped fresh flat-leaf parsley
- 2 tbsp lemon juice
- 8–10 radicchio leaves
- salt and pepper

1 Bring a large saucepan of lightly salted water to a boil. Add the green beans, reduce the heat, and cook for 5–6 minutes. Remove with a slotted spoon and refresh in a bowl of cold water. Drain well. Add the pasta to the same saucepan, return to a boil, and cook for 8–10 minutes, or until tender but still firm to the bite.

2 Meanwhile, brush a grill pan with some of the olive oil and heat until smoking. Season the tuna to taste with salt and pepper and brush both sides with some of the remaining olive oil. Cook over medium heat for 2 minutes on each side, or until cooked to your liking, then remove from the grill pan and reserve.

3 Drain the pasta well and transfer it to a bowl. Add the green beans, cherry tomatoes, olives, anchovies, parsley, lemon juice, and remaining olive oil and season to taste with salt and pepper. Toss well and let cool. Remove and discard any skin from the tuna and slice thickly.

4 Gently mix the tuna into the pasta salad. Line a serving bowl with the radicchio leaves, spoon the salad on top, and serve.

tuna & herbed fusilli salad

serves 4

- 7 oz/200 g dried fusilli (pasta spirals)
- 1 red bell pepper, seeded and quartered
- 5½ oz/150 g asparagus spears
- 1 red onion, sliced
- 4 tomatoes, sliced
- 7 oz/200 g canned tuna in brine, drained and flaked
- salt

dressing

- 6 tbsp basil-flavored oil or extra virgin olive oil
- 3 tbsp white wine vinegar
- 1 tbsp lime juice
- 1 tsp mustard
- 1 tsp honey
- 4 tbsp chopped fresh basil, plus extra sprigs to garnish

1 Bring a large saucepan of lightly salted water to a boil. Add the pasta, return to a boil, and cook for 8–10 minutes, or until tender but still firm to the bite.

2 Meanwhile, put the bell pepper quarters under a preheated hot broiler and cook for 10–12 minutes until the skins begin to blacken. Transfer to a plastic bag, seal, and set aside.

3 Bring a separate saucepan of water to a boil, add the asparagus, and blanch for 4 minutes. Drain and plunge into cold water, then drain again. Remove the pasta from the heat, drain, and set aside to cool. Remove the pepper quarters from the bag and peel off the skins. Slice the pepper into strips.

4 To make the dressing, put all the dressing ingredients in a serving bowl and stir together well. Add the pasta, pepper strips, asparagus, onion, tomatoes, and tuna. Toss together gently, garnish with basil sprigs, and serve.

Mmmm...
meat & poultry

spaghetti bolognese

serves 4

- 1 tbsp olive oil
- 1 onion, finely chopped
- 2 garlic cloves, chopped
- 1 carrot, chopped
- 1 celery stalk, chopped
- 1¾ oz/50 g pancetta or bacon, diced
- 12 oz/350 g lean ground beef
- 14 oz/400 g canned chopped tomatoes
- 2 tsp dried oregano
- ½ cup red wine
- 2 tbsp tomato paste
- 12 oz/350 g dried spaghetti
- salt and pepper
- chopped fresh flat-leaf parsley, to garnish

1 Heat the oil in a large skillet. Add the onion and cook for 3 minutes. Add the garlic, carrot, celery, and pancetta and cook for 3–4 minutes, or until just beginning to brown.

2 Add the beef and cook over high heat for an additional 3 minutes, or until the meat has browned. Stir in the tomatoes, oregano, and red wine and bring to a boil. Reduce the heat and simmer for about 45 minutes.

3 Stir in the tomato paste and season to taste with salt and pepper.

4 Meanwhile, bring a large saucepan of lightly salted water to a boil. Add the pasta, return to a boil, and cook for 8–10 minutes, or until tender but still firm to the bite.

5 Transfer the spaghetti to a warmed serving dish and pour over the bolognese sauce. Toss to mix well, garnish with parsley, and serve.

spaghetti with meatballs

serves 6

- 1 potato, diced
- 14 oz/400 g ground steak
- 1 onion, finely chopped
- 1 egg
- 4 tbsp chopped fresh flat-leaf parsley
- all-purpose flour, for dusting
- 5 tbsp olive oil
- 1¾ cups strained canned tomatoes
- 2 tbsp tomato paste
- 14 oz/400 g dried spaghetti
- salt and pepper
- fresh basil leaves, to garnish
- fresh Parmesan cheese shavings, to serve

1 Place the potato in a small saucepan, add cold water to cover and a pinch of salt, and bring to a boil. Cook for 10–15 minutes, until tender, then drain. Mash thoroughly with a potato masher.

2 Combine the potato, steak, onion, egg, and parsley in a bowl and season to taste with salt and pepper. Spread out the flour on a plate. With dampened hands, shape the meat mixture into walnut-size balls and roll in the flour.

3 Heat the olive oil in a heavy-bottom skillet, add the meatballs, and cook over medium heat, stirring and turning frequently, for 8–10 minutes. Add the strained tomatoes and tomato paste and cook for an additional 10 minutes, or until the sauce is reduced and thickened.

4 Meanwhile, bring a large saucepan of lightly salted water to a boil. Add the pasta, return to a boil, and cook for 8–10 minutes, or until tender but still firm to the bite.

5 Drain well and add to the meatball sauce, tossing well to coat. Transfer to a warmed serving dish, garnish with the basil, and serve with the Parmesan.

spaghetti alla carbonara

serves 4

- 14 oz/400 g dried spaghetti
- 4 eggs
- 4 tbsp heavy cream
- ½ cup grated Parmesan cheese
- ½ cup grated pecorino cheese
- 1 tbsp butter
- 150 g/5½ oz pancetta, diced
- salt and pepper

1 Bring a large saucepan of lightly salted water to a boil. Add the pasta, return to a boil, and cook for 8–10 minutes, or until tender but still firm to the bite.

2 Meanwhile, beat the eggs in a bowl with the cream, cheeses, and salt and pepper to taste. Melt the butter in a large, deep skillet and fry the pancetta until crispy.

3 Drain the pasta, but not too thoroughly, then add to the skillet and pour over the egg mixture. Remove from the heat and stir until the egg mixture is warmed through but still creamy.

4 Transfer to a warmed serving dish, add extra seasoning, if liked, and serve.

pepperoni pasta

serves 4

- 3 tbsp olive oil
- 1 onion, chopped
- 1 red bell pepper, seeded and diced
- 1 orange bell pepper, seeded and diced
- 1 lb 12 oz/800 g canned chopped tomatoes
- 1 tbsp sun-dried tomato paste
- 1 tsp paprika
- 8 oz/225 g pepperoni sausage, sliced
- 2 tbsp chopped fresh flat-leaf parsley, plus extra to garnish
- 1 lb/450 g dried penne (pasta quills)
- salt and pepper

1 Heat 2 tablespoons of the oil in a large, heavy-bottom skillet over a medium heat. Add the onion and cook, stirring occasionally, for 5 minutes, or until softened. Stir in the red and orange bell peppers, tomatoes with their juices, sun-dried tomato paste, and paprika and bring to a boil.

2 Add the pepperoni and parsley and season to taste with salt and pepper. Stir well and bring to a boil, then reduce the heat and simmer for 10–15 minutes.

3 Meanwhile, bring a large saucepan of lightly salted water to a boil. Add the pasta, return to a boil, and cook for 8–10 minutes, or until tender but still firm to the bite. Drain well and transfer to a warmed serving dish. Add the remaining oil and toss to coat. Add the sauce and toss again. Sprinkle with parsley to garnish and serve.

farfalle with bleu cheese & ham

serves 4

- 1 cup crème fraîche or sour cream
- 8 oz/225 g cremini mushrooms, quartered
- 14 oz/400 g dried farfalle (pasta bows)
- 3 oz/85 g bleu cheese, crumbled
- 1 tbsp chopped fresh flat-leaf parsley, plus extra sprigs to garnish
- 1 cup cooked ham, diced
- salt and pepper

1 Pour the crème fraîche into a saucepan, add the mushrooms, and season to taste with salt and pepper. Bring to just below a boil, then lower the heat, and simmer gently, stirring occasionally, for 8–10 minutes, until the cream has thickened.

2 Meanwhile, bring a large saucepan of lightly salted water to a boil. Add the pasta, return to a boil, and cook for 8–10 minutes, or until tender but still firm to the bite.

3 Remove the saucepan of mushrooms from the heat and stir in the bleu cheese until it has melted. Return the pan to low heat and stir in the chopped parsley and ham.

4 Drain the pasta and add it to the sauce. Transfer to a warmed serving dish, garnish with sprigs of parsley, and serve with extra pepper, if liked.

penne with ham, tomato & chile

serves 4

- 1 tbsp olive oil
- 2 tbsp butter
- 1 onion, finely chopped
- ⅔ cup diced ham
- 2 garlic cloves, very finely chopped
- 1 red chile, seeded and finely chopped
- 1 lb 12 oz/800 g canned chopped tomatoes
- 1 lb/450 g dried penne (pasta quills)
- 2 tbsp chopped fresh flat-leaf parsley
- 6 tbsp freshly grated Parmesan cheese, plus extra to serve
- salt and pepper

1 Put the olive oil and 1 tablespoon of the butter in a large skillet over medium–low heat. Add the onion and cook for 10 minutes, or until soft and golden. Add the ham and cook for an additional 5 minutes, or until lightly browned. Stir in the garlic, chile, and tomatoes. Season to taste with salt and pepper. Bring to a boil, then simmer over medium–low heat for 30–40 minutes, or until thickened.

2 Meanwhile, bring a large saucepan of lightly salted water to a boil. Add the pasta, return to a boil, and cook for 8–10 minutes, or until tender but still firm to the bite. Drain and transfer to a warmed serving dish.

3 Pour the sauce over the pasta. Add the parsley, Parmesan cheese, and the remaining butter. Toss well to mix, top with extra grated Parmesan, and serve.

rigatoni with spicy sausage

serves 4

- 4 tbsp olive oil
- 1 red onion, chopped
- 1 garlic clove, chopped
- 1 celery stalk, sliced
- 14 oz/400 g dried rigatoni (pasta tubes)
- 10 oz/280 g spicy sausage, sliced
- 8 oz/225 g cremini mushrooms, halved
- 1 tbsp chopped fresh cilantro
- 1 tbsp lime juice
- salt and pepper

1 Heat the oil in a skillet. Add the onion, garlic, and celery and cook over low heat, stirring occasionally, for 5 minutes, until softened.

2 Meanwhile, bring a large saucepan of lightly salted water to a boil. Add the pasta, return to a boil, and cook for 8–10 minutes, or until tender but still firm to the bite.

3 While the pasta is cooking, add the sausage to the skillet and cook, stirring occasionally, for 5 minutes, until evenly browned. Add the mushrooms and cook, stirring occasionally, for an additional 5 minutes. Stir in the cilantro and lime juice and season to taste with salt and pepper.

4 Drain the pasta and return it to the saucepan. Add the sausage-and-mushroom mixture and toss lightly. Transfer to a warmed serving dish and serve.

macaroni with sausage & olives

serves 6

- 1 tbsp olive oil
- 1 large onion, finely chopped
- 2 garlic cloves, finely chopped
- 1 lb/450 g pork sausage, peeled and coarsely chopped
- 3 canned pepperoncini, or other hot red peppers, drained and sliced
- 14 oz/400 g canned chopped tomatoes
- 2 tsp dried oregano
- ½ cup chicken stock or red wine
- 1 lb/450 g dried macaroni
- 12–15 pitted black olives, cut into quarters
- ⅔ cup freshly grated cheese, such as Gruyère
- salt and pepper

1 Heat the oil in a large skillet over medium heat. Add the onion and cook for 5 minutes, until soft. Add the garlic and cook for a few seconds, until just beginning to color. Add the sausage and cook until evenly browned.

2 Stir in the pepperoncini, tomatoes, oregano, and stock. Season to taste with salt and pepper. Bring to a boil, then simmer over medium heat for 10 minutes, stirring occasionally.

3 Meanwhile, bring a large saucepan of lightly salted water to a boil. Add the pasta, return to a boil, and cook for 8–10 minutes, or until tender but still firm to the bite. Drain and transfer to a warmed serving dish. Keep warm.

4 Add the olives and half the cheese to the sauce, then stir until the cheese has melted.

5 Pour the sauce over the pasta. Toss well to mix and transfer to a warmed serving dish. Sprinkle with the remaining cheese and serve.

penne with sausage sauce

serves 4–6

- 2 tbsp olive oil
- 1 red onion, coarsely chopped
- 2 garlic cloves, coarsely chopped
- 6 Italian sausages, skinned and the meat crumbled
- ½ tsp dried chile flakes
- 2 tbsp chopped fresh oregano
- 14 oz/400 g canned chopped tomatoes
- 12 oz/350 g dried penne (pasta quills)
- salt and pepper
- chopped fresh flat-leaf parsley, to garnish
- freshly grated Parmesan cheese, to serve

1 Heat the oil in a large pan, add the onion, and cook over medium heat, stirring frequently, for 6–8 minutes, or until starting to brown. Add the garlic and the crumbled sausages and cook for 8–10 minutes, breaking up the sausages with a wooden spoon.

2 Add the chile flakes and oregano and stir well. Pour in the tomatoes and bring to a boil, then reduce the heat and simmer, uncovered, for 4–5 minutes, or until reduced and thickened. Season to taste with salt and pepper.

3 Meanwhile, bring a large saucepan of lightly salted water to a boil. Add the pasta, return to a boil, and cook for 8–10 minutes, or until tender but still firm to the bite. Drain well and return to the saucepan.

4 Pour the sauce into the pasta and stir well. Transfer to a warmed serving dish, garnish with parsley, and serve with the Parmesan.

fusilli with bacon, eggs & mushrooms

serves 6

- 1 tbsp olive oil
- 4 strips lean bacon or pancetta
- 2 cups mushrooms, sliced
- 8 oz/225 g dried fusilli (pasta spirals)
- 2 eggs, beaten
- scant 1 cup cubed cheddar or mozzarella cheese
- salt and pepper
- chopped fresh flat-leaf parsley, to garnish

1 Heat the oil in a skillet over a medium heat. Add the bacon and cook until crisp. Remove with tongs, cut into small pieces, and keep warm.

2 Cook the mushrooms in the pan with the bacon fat for 5–7 minutes, or until soft. Remove from the heat.

3 Meanwhile, bring a large saucepan of lightly salted water to a boil. Add the pasta, return to a boil, and cook for 8–10 minutes, or until tender but still firm to the bite. Drain.

4 Stir the mushrooms, eggs, and the cheese cubes into the pasta. Season with pepper and toss until the eggs have coated the pasta and the cheese has melted.

5 Transfer to a warmed serving dish. Sprinkle with the bacon pieces and parsley and serve.

tagliatelle with spring lamb

serves 4

- 1 lb 10 oz/750 g boneless lean lamb in a single piece
- 6 garlic cloves, thinly sliced
- 6–8 fresh rosemary sprigs
- ½ cup olive oil
- 14 oz/400 g dried tagliatelle (thick pasta stands)
- 4 tbsp butter
- 6 oz/175 g white mushrooms
- salt and pepper
- freshly shaved Romano cheese, to serve

1 Using a sharp knife, cut small pockets all over the lamb, then insert a garlic slice and a few rosemary leaves in each one. Heat 2 tablespoons of the olive oil in a large, heavy-bottom skillet. Add the lamb and cook over medium heat, turning occasionally, for 25–30 minutes, until tender and cooked to your liking.

2 Meanwhile, chop the remaining rosemary and place in a mortar. Add the remaining oil and pound with a pestle. Season to taste.

3 Remove the lamb from the heat, cover with foil, and let stand. Bring a large saucepan of salted water to a boil. Add the pasta, return to a boil, and cook for 8–10 minutes, or until tender but still firm to the bite.

4 Meanwhile, melt the butter in another pan. Add the mushrooms and cook over medium–low heat, stirring occasionally, for 5–8 minutes, until tender.

5 Drain the pasta, return it to the saucepan, and toss with half the rosemary oil. Slice the lamb. Transfer the pasta to a warmed serving dish, season with pepper, and top with the lamb and mushrooms. Drizzle with the remaining rosemary oil, sprinkle with the cheese, and serve.

quick pork & pasta stir-fry

serves 4

- 14 oz/400 g dried fettucine (thick pasta strands)
- 1 tbsp peanut oil
- ½ tsp chili powder, or to taste
- 2 garlic cloves, crushed
- ½ red cabbage, shredded
- 2 leeks, sliced thinly
- 1 orange bell pepper, sliced thinly
- 1 carrot, sliced thinly
- 1 zucchini, sliced thinly
- 12 oz/350 g pork tenderloin, cubed
- salt

1 Bring a large saucepan of lightly salted water to a boil. Add the pasta, return to a boil, and cook for 8–10 minutes, or until tender but still firm to the bite. Drain well and return to the saucepan.

2 Meanwhile, heat the oil in a wok or large skillet over medium heat and add the chili powder, garlic, and red cabbage. Stir-fry for 2–3 minutes.

3 Stir in the rest of the vegetables and cook for another 2 minutes. Add the meat, then increase the heat and stir-fry for 5 minutes, or until the pork is well cooked and the dish is piping hot.

4 Place the pasta in a warmed serving dish, add the stir-fry mixture, and serve.

pappardelle with chicken

serves 4

- ½ cup dried porcini mushrooms
- ¾ cup hot water
- 1 lb 12 oz/800 g canned chopped tomatoes
- 1 fresh red chile, seeded and finely chopped
- 3 tbsp olive oil
- 12 oz/350 g skinless, boneless chicken, cut into thin strips
- 2 garlic cloves, finely chopped
- 12 oz/350 g dried pappardelle (thick pasta strands)
- salt and pepper
- chopped fresh flat-leaf parsley, to garnish

1 Place the porcini in a small bowl, add the hot water, and let soak for 20 minutes. Meanwhile, place the tomatoes and their juices in a heavy-bottom pan and stir in the chile. Bring to a boil, reduce the heat, and simmer, stirring occasionally, for 30 minutes, or until reduced.

2 Remove the mushrooms from their soaking liquid, reserving the liquid. Strain the liquid through a cheesecloth-lined strainer into the tomatoes and simmer for an additional 15 minutes. Meanwhile, heat 2 tablespoons of the oil in a heavy-bottom skillet. Add the chicken and cook, stirring frequently, until golden brown all over and tender. Stir in the mushrooms and garlic and cook for an additional 5 minutes.

3 Meanwhile, bring a large saucepan of lightly salted water to a boil. Add the pasta, return to a boil, and cook for 8–10 minutes, or until tender but still firm to the bite. Drain well, transfer to a warmed serving dish, drizzle with the remaining oil, and toss lightly. Stir the chicken mixture into the tomato sauce, season to taste with salt and pepper, and spoon onto the pasta. Toss lightly, sprinkle with parsley, and serve.

fettuccine with chicken & pesto

serves 4

- 2 tbsp vegetable oil
- 4 skinless, boneless chicken breasts
- 12 oz/350 g dried fettuccine (thick pasta stands)
- salt and pepper
- sprig of fresh basil, to garnish

pesto

- 1⅔ cups shredded fresh basil
- ½ cup extra virgin olive oil
- 3 tbsp pine nuts
- 3 garlic cloves, crushed
- ½ cup freshly grated Parmesan cheese

1 To make the pesto, put the basil, olive oil, pine nuts, garlic, and a generous pinch of salt in a food processor or blender. Process the ingredients until smooth. Scrape the mixture into a bowl and stir in the cheese.

2 Heat the vegetable oil in a skillet over medium heat. Cook the chicken breasts, turning once, for 8–10 minutes, or until the juices are no longer pink. Cut into small cubes.

3 Meanwhile, bring a large saucepan of lightly salted water to a boil. Add the pasta, return to a boil, and cook for 8–10 minutes, or until tender but still firm to the bite. Drain and transfer to a warmed serving dish. Add the chicken and pesto, then season to taste with pepper. Toss well to mix.

4 Transfer to a warmed serving dish, garnish with a sprig of basil, and serve.

chicken with linguine & artichokes

serves 4

- 4 chicken breasts, skinless, boneless chicken breasts
- finely grated rind and juice of 1 lemon
- 2 tbsp olive oil
- 10½ oz/300 g dried linguine (thin pasta strands)
- 2 garlic cloves, crushed
- 14 oz/400 g canned artichoke hearts, drained and sliced
- 9 oz/250 g baby plum tomatoes
- salt
- chopped fresh flat-leaf parsley, to garnish
- freshly grated Parmesan cheese, to serve

1 Put each chicken breast between 2 pieces of plastic wrap and pound lightly to flatten. Put the chicken into a shallow, nonmetallic dish with the lemon rind and juice and 1 tablespoon of the oil and turn to coat in the marinade. Cover and let marinate in the refrigerator for 30 minutes.

2 Meanwhile, bring a large saucepan of lightly salted water to a boil. Add the pasta, return to a boil, and cook for 8–10 minutes, or until tender but still firm to the bite. Heat the remaining oil in a skillet over low heat, add the garlic, and cook for 1 minute, stirring frequently. Add the artichokes and tomatoes and cook for 5 minutes, stirring occasionally. Add about half the marinade from the chicken and cook over medium heat for an additional 5 minutes.

3 Meanwhile, preheat the broiler to high. Remove the chicken from the remaining marinade and arrange on the broiler pan. Cook the chicken under the preheated broiler for about 5 minutes each side, until thoroughly cooked. Drain the pasta and return to the pan, pour over the artichoke-and-tomato mixture, and slice in the cooked chicken.

4 Transfer to a warmed serving dish, garnish with the parsley, and serve with the Parmesan.

spaghetti with parsley chicken

serves 4

- 1 tbsp olive oil
- thinly pared rind of 1 lemon, cut into julienne strips
- 1 tsp finely chopped fresh ginger
- 1 tsp sugar
- 1 cup chicken stock
- 9 oz/250 g dried spaghetti
- 4 tbsp butter
- 8 oz/225 g skinless, boneless chicken breasts, diced
- 1 red onion, finely chopped
- leaves from 2 bunches of fresh flat-leaf parsley
- salt and pepper

1 Heat the oil in a heavy-bottom pan. Add the lemon rind and cook over low heat, stirring frequently, for 5 minutes. Stir in the ginger and sugar, season to taste with salt, and cook, stirring constantly, for an additional 2 minutes. Pour in the chicken stock, bring to a boil, then cook for 5 minutes, or until the liquid has reduced by half.

2 Meanwhile, bring a large saucepan of lightly salted water to a boil. Add the pasta, return to a boil, and cook for 8–10 minutes, or until tender but still firm to the bite.

3 Melt half the butter in a skillet. Add the chicken and onion and cook, stirring frequently, for 5 minutes, or until the chicken is lightly browned all over. Stir in the lemon-and-ginger mixture and cook for 1 minute. Stir in the parsley leaves and cook, stirring constantly, for an additional 3 minutes.

4 Drain the pasta and transfer to a warmed serving dish, then add the remaining butter and toss well. Stir in the chicken sauce, add extra seasoning, if liked, and serve.

chicken with creamy penne

serves 2

- 7 oz/200 g dried penne (pasta quills)
- 1 tbsp olive oil
- 2 skinless, boneless chicken breasts
- 4 tbsp dry white wine
- generous 1 cup frozen peas
- 5 tbsp heavy cream
- salt
- chopped fresh parsley, to garnish

1 Bring a large saucepan of lightly salted water to a boil. Add the pasta, return to a boil, and cook for 8–10 minutes, or until tender but still firm to the bite.

2 Meanwhile, heat the oil in a skillet, add the chicken, and cook over medium heat for about 4 minutes on each side.

3 Pour in the wine and cook over high heat until it has almost evaporated.

4 Drain the pasta. Add the peas, cream, and pasta to the skillet and stir well. Cover and simmer for 2 minutes.

5 Garnish with the parsley and serve.

farfalle with chicken, broccoli & peppers

serves 4

- 4 tbsp olive oil
- 5 tbsp butter
- 3 garlic cloves, finely chopped
- 1 lb/450 g boneless, skinless chicken breasts, diced
- ¼ tsp dried chile flakes
- 1 lb/450 g small broccoli florets
- 10½ oz/300 g dried farfalle (pasta bows)
- 6 oz/175 g jar roasted red bell peppers, drained and diced
- 1 cup chicken stock
- salt and pepper

1 Bring a large saucepan of lightly salted water to a boil. Meanwhile, heat the oil and butter in a large skillet over medium–low heat. Add the garlic and cook until just beginning to color.

2 Add the diced chicken, then raise the heat to medium and cook for 4–5 minutes, or until the chicken is no longer pink. Add the chile flakes and season to taste with salt and pepper. Remove from the heat.

3 Plunge the broccoli into the boiling water and cook for 2 minutes. Remove with a slotted spoon and set aside. Bring the water back to a boil. Add the pasta and cook for 8–10 minutes, or until tender but still firm to the bite. Drain and add to the chicken mixture in the pan. Add the broccoli and roasted bell peppers. Pour in the stock. Simmer briskly over medium–high heat, stirring frequently, until most of the liquid has been absorbed.

4 Transfer to a warmed serving dish and serve.

tagliatelle with lemon turkey

serves 4

- 1 lb/450 g turkey breast, cut into strips
- 14 oz/400 g dried tagliatelle (thick pasta strands)
- 1 tbsp vegetable oil
- 6 scallions, finely sliced
- ½ lemon, peeled and thinly sliced
- 1 garlic clove, finely chopped
- 10½ oz/300 g spinach, washed, drained, and coarsely chopped
- 3 tbsp chopped fresh flat-leaf parsley
- salt and pepper
- lemon slices, to garnish
- sprigs of flat-leaf parsley, to garnish

marinade

- 1 tbsp soy sauce
- 1 tbsp white wine vinegar
- 1 tsp cornstarch
- 1 tsp finely grated lemon zest

1 To make the marinade, put the soy sauce, vinegar, cornstarch, lemon zest, and pepper to taste in a bowl and mix thoroughly. Add the turkey and stir to coat. Cover with plastic wrap and marinate in the refrigerator for 30 minutes.

2 Bring a large saucepan of lightly salted water to a boil. Add the pasta, return to a boil, and cook for about 8–10 minutes, or until tender and still firm to the bite.

3 Heat the oil in a large wok or skillet. Add the turkey and the marinade and cook over medium heat for 2–3 minutes, or until the turkey is opaque.

4 Add the scallions, lemon slices, and garlic and cook for an additional 2–3 minutes. Stir in the spinach and parsley and cook until the spinach is just wilted.

5 Drain the pasta and transfer to a warmed serving dish. Remove the scallion mixture from the heat, spoon over the pasta, and garnish with sprigs of parsley and lemon slices before serving.

penne with turkey meatballs

serves 4

- 12 oz/350 g ground turkey
- 1 small garlic clove, finely chopped
- 2 tbsp finely chopped fresh parsley
- 1 egg, lightly beaten
- all-purpose flour, for dusting
- 3 tbsp olive oil
- 1 onion, finely chopped
- 1 celery stalk, finely chopped
- 1 carrot, finely chopped
- 14 oz/400 g strained canned tomatoes
- 1 fresh rosemary sprig
- 1 bay leaf
- 12 oz/350 g dried penne (pasta quills)
- salt and pepper
- freshly grated Parmesan cheese, to serve

1 Put the turkey, garlic, and parsley in a bowl and mix well. Stir in the egg and season to taste with salt and pepper. Dust your hands lightly with flour and shape the mixture into walnut-size balls between your palms. Lightly dust each meatball with flour.

2 Heat the olive oil in a saucepan. Add the onion, celery, and carrot and cook over low heat, stirring occasionally, for 5 minutes, until softened. Increase the heat to medium, add the meatballs, and cook, turning frequently, for 8–10 minutes, until golden brown all over.

3 Pour in the strained canned tomatoes, add the rosemary and bay leaf, season to taste with salt and pepper, and bring to a boil. Lower the heat, cover, and simmer gently, stirring occasionally, for 40–45 minutes. Remove and discard the herbs.

4 Shortly before the meatballs are ready, bring a large saucepan of salted water to a boil. Add the pasta, return to a boil, and cook for 8–10 minutes, or until tender but still firm to the bite. Drain and add to the pan with the meatballs. Stir gently and heat through briefly, then spoon into warmed serving dishes. Sprinkle generously with the Parmesan and serve.

Mmmm...
fish & seafood

spaghetti alla puttanesca

serves 4

- 3 tbsp olive oil
- 2 garlic cloves, finely chopped
- 10 canned anchovy fillets, drained and chopped
- 1 cup pitted and chopped black olives
- 1 tbsp drained and rinsed capers
- 1 lb/450 g plum tomatoes, peeled, seeded, and chopped
- pinch of cayenne pepper
- 14 oz/400 g dried spaghetti
- salt
- chopped fresh flat-leaf parsley, to garnish

1 Heat the oil in a heavy-bottom skillet. Add the garlic and cook over low heat, stirring frequently, for 2 minutes. Add the anchovies and mash them to a pulp with a fork. Add the olives, capers, and tomatoes, and season to taste with cayenne pepper. Cover and simmer for 25 minutes.

2 Meanwhile, bring a large saucepan of lightly salted water to a boil. Add the pasta, return to a boil, and cook for 8–10 minutes, or until tender but still firm to the bite. Drain well and transfer to a warmed serving dish.

3 Spoon the anchovy sauce into the dish and toss the pasta, using 2 large forks. Garnish with the chopped parsley, and serve.

linguine with sardines

serves 4

- 8 sardines, filleted, washed, and dried
- 4 tbsp olive oil
- 3 garlic cloves, sliced
- 1 tsp chile flakes
- 1 fennel bulb, trimmed and thinly sliced
- 12 oz/350 g dried linguine (thin pasta strands)
- ½ tsp finely grated lemon rind
- 1 tbsp lemon juice
- 2 tbsp toasted pine nuts
- 2 tbsp chopped fresh parsley
- salt and pepper

1 Roughly chop the sardines into large pieces and reserve.

2 Heat 2 tablespoons of the oil in a large skillet over medium–high heat and add the garlic and chile flakes.

3 Cook for 1 minute, then add the fennel. Cook, stirring occasionally, for 4–5 minutes, or until softened.

4 Reduce the heat, add the sardine pieces, and cook for an additional 3–4 minutes.

5 Meanwhile, bring a large saucepan of lightly salted water to a boil. Add the pasta, return to a boil, and cook for 8–10 minutes, or until tender but still firm to the bite. Drain thoroughly and return to the pan. Keep warm.

6 Add the lemon rind, lemon juice, pine nuts, and parsley to the sardine mixture and toss together. Season to taste with salt and pepper.

7 Add to the pasta with the remaining oil and toss together gently. Transfer to a warmed serving dish, add extra seasoning, if liked, and serve.

penne with sicilian sauce

serves 4

- ½ cup golden raisins
- 1 lb/450 g tomatoes, halved
- ¼ cup pine nuts
- 1¾ oz/50 g canned anchovies, drained and halved lengthwise
- 2 tbsp tomato paste
- 12 oz/350 g dried penne (pasta quills)
- salt and pepper

1 Soak the golden raisins in a bowl of warm water for about 20 minutes. Drain thoroughly.

2 Preheat the broiler, then cook the tomatoes under the hot broiler for 10 minutes. Let cool slightly, then once cool enough to handle, peel off the skin and dice the flesh. Place the pine nuts on a cookie sheet and lightly toast under the broiler for 2–3 minutes, or until golden brown.

3 Place the tomatoes, pine nuts, and golden raisins in a small pan and heat gently. Add the anchovies and tomato paste, and cook the sauce over low heat for an additional 2–3 minutes, or until hot.

4 Meanwhile, bring a large saucepan of lightly salted water to a boil. Add the pasta, return to a boil, and cook for 8–10 minutes, or until tender but still firm to the bite. Drain thoroughly, transfer the pasta to a warmed serving dish, and add the sauce. Add extra seasoning, if liked, and serve.

fettuccine with spinach & anchovies

serves 4

- 2 lb/900 g fresh baby spinach leaves
- 14 oz/400 g dried fettuccine (thick pasta strands)
- 5 tbsp olive oil
- 3 tbsp pine nuts
- 3 garlic cloves, crushed
- 8 canned anchovy fillets, drained and chopped
- salt

1 Trim off any tough spinach stalks. Rinse the spinach leaves under cold running water and place them in a large saucepan with only the water that is clinging to them after washing. Cover and cook over high heat, shaking the saucepan from time to time, until the spinach has wilted but retains its color. Drain well, set aside, and keep warm.

2 Bring a large saucepan of lightly salted water to a boil. Add the pasta, return to a boil, and cook for 8–10 minutes, or until tender but still firm to the bite.

3 Heat 4 tablespoons of the oil in a separate saucepan. Add the pine nuts and cook until golden. Remove the pine nuts from the saucepan and set aside until needed.

4 Add the garlic to the saucepan and cook until golden. Add the anchovies and stir in the spinach. Cook, stirring, for 2–3 minutes, until heated through. Return the pine nuts to the saucepan.

5 Drain the fettuccine, toss in the remaining oil, and transfer to a warmed serving dish. Spoon the anchovy-and-spinach sauce over the fettuccine, toss lightly, and serve.

spaghetti con vongole

serves 4

- 2 lb 4 oz/1 kg clams, scrubbed
- 3/4 cup water
- 3/4 cup dry white wine
- 12 oz/350 g dried spaghetti
- 5 tbsp olive oil
- 2 garlic cloves, finely chopped
- 4 tbsp chopped fresh flat-leaf parsley
- salt and pepper

1 Discard any clams with broken shells or any that refuse to close when tapped. Place the clams in a large, heavy-bottom pan. Add the water and wine, then cover and cook over high heat, shaking the pan occasionally, for 5 minutes, or until the shells have opened. Remove the clams with a slotted spoon and strain the liquid through a cheesecloth-lined strainer into a small pan. Bring to a boil and cook until reduced by about half. Discard any clams that remain closed and remove the remainder from their shells.

2 Bring a large saucepan of lightly salted water to a boil. Add the pasta, return to a boil, and cook for 8–10 minutes, or until tender but still firm to the bite.

3 Meanwhile, heat the olive oil in a large, heavy-bottom skillet. Add the garlic and cook, stirring frequently, for 2 minutes. Add the parsley and the reduced cooking liquid and simmer gently. Drain the pasta and add it to the skillet with the clams. Season to taste with salt and pepper and cook, stirring constantly, for 4 minutes, or until the pasta is coated and the clams have heated through. Transfer to a warmed serving dish and serve.

sea bass with olive sauce

serves 4

- 1 lb/450 g dried macaroni
- 8 sea bass fillets, 4 oz/115 g each
- salt and pepper
- shredded leek, to garnish
- shredded carrot, to garnish

sauce

- 2 tbsp butter
- 4 shallots, chopped
- 2 tbsp capers
- 1½ cups chopped, pitted green olives
- 4 tbsp balsamic vinegar
- 1¼ cups fish stock
- 1¼ cups heavy cream
- juice of 1 lemon

1 To make the sauce, melt the butter in a skillet. Add the shallots and cook over a low heat for 4 minutes. Add the capers and olives and cook for an additional 3 minutes.

2 Stir in the balsamic vinegar and fish stock. Bring to a boil and reduce by half. Add the cream, stirring, and reduce again by half. Season to taste with salt and pepper and stir in the lemon juice. Remove the pan from the heat; set aside and keep warm.

3 Bring a large saucepan of lightly salted water to a boil. Add the pasta, return to a boil, and cook for 8–10 minutes, or until tender but still firm to the bite.

4 Meanwhile, lightly broil the sea bass fillets for 3–4 minutes on each side, until cooked through but still moist and delicate.

5 Drain the pasta thoroughly and transfer to warmed serving dishes. Top the pasta with the fish fillets and pour the olive sauce over. Garnish with shredded leek and carrot and serve.

creamy smoked trout tagliatelle

serves 6

- 2 carrots, cut into thin sticks
- 2 celery stalks, cut into thin sticks
- 1 zucchini, cut into thin sticks
- 1 leek, cut into thin sticks
- 1 cup fresh or frozen peas
- ⅔ cup vegetable stock
- 8 oz/225 g smoked trout fillets, skinned and cut into thin strips
- scant 1 cup cream cheese
- ⅔ cup dry white wine
- 2 tbsp chopped fresh dill, plus extra sprigs to garnish
- 8 oz/225 g dried tagliatelle (thick pasta strands)
- salt and pepper

1 Put the carrots, celery, zucchini, leek, and peas in a large saucepan and pour in the stock. Bring to a boil, then reduce the heat and let simmer for 5 minutes, or until the vegetables are tender and most of the stock has evaporated. Remove the pan from the heat, stir in the smoked trout, and cover to keep warm.

2 Put the cheese and wine in a separate saucepan over low heat and stir until the cheese has melted and the mixture is smooth. Stir in the chopped dill and season to taste with salt and pepper.

3 Meanwhile, bring a large saucepan of lightly salted water to a boil. Add the pasta, return to a boil, and cook for 8–10 minutes, until tender but still firm to the bite. Drain the pasta and add to the cheese sauce. Toss the pasta using 2 large forks, then transfer to a warmed serving dish. Top with the smoked trout mixture, garnish with dill sprigs, and serve.

fusilli with monkfish & broccoli

serves 4

- 1⅔ cups small broccoli florets
- 3 tbsp olive oil
- 12 oz/350 g monkfish fillet, skinned and cut into bite-size pieces
- 2 garlic cloves, crushed
- ½ cup dry white wine
- 1 cup heavy cream
- 14 oz/400 g dried fusilli (pasta spirals)
- 3 oz/85 g bleu cheese, diced
- salt and pepper

1 Bring a saucepan of lightly salted water to a boil, add the broccoli, and cook for 2 minutes. Drain and refresh under cold running water.

2 Heat the olive oil in a large heavy-bottom skillet. Add the monkfish and garlic and season to taste with salt and pepper. Cook, stirring frequently, for 5 minutes, or until the fish is opaque. Pour in the white wine and cream and cook, stirring occasionally, for 5 minutes, or until the fish is cooked through and the sauce has thickened. Stir in the broccoli.

3 Meanwhile, bring a large saucepan of lightly salted water to a boil. Add the pasta, return to a boil, and cook for 8–10 minutes, or until tender but still firm to the bite. Drain and turn the pasta into the pan with the fish, add the cheese, and toss lightly. Transfer to a warmed serving dish, add extra seasoning if liked, and serve.

spaghetti with salmon & arugula

serves 4

- 12 oz/350 g dried spaghetti
- 2 tbsp olive oil
- 1 garlic clove, finely chopped
- 4 oz/115 g smoked salmon, cut into thin strips
- 2¾ cups arugula
- salt and pepper

1 Bring a large saucepan of lightly salted water to a boil. Add the pasta, return to a boil, and cook for 8–10 minutes, or until tender but still firm to the bite.

2 Just before the end of the cooking time, heat the olive oil in a heavy-bottom skillet. Add the garlic and cook over low heat, stirring constantly, for 1 minute. Add the salmon and arugula. Season to taste with salt and pepper and cook, stirring constantly, for 1 minute. Remove the skillet from the heat.

3 Drain the pasta and transfer to a warmed serving dish. Add the smoked salmon-and-arugula mixture, toss lightly, and serve.

creamy salmon pasta

serves 4

- 9 oz/250 g dried fusilli (pasta spirals)
- 2¾ cups small broccoli florets
- 9 oz /250 g skinless salmon fillet
- scant ½ cup plain yogurt
- 2 tbsp milk
- 4 tbsp freshly grated Parmesan cheese
- 2 tsp smooth Dijon mustard
- salt and pepper
- chopped fresh flat-leaf parsley, for garnish

1 Bring a large saucepan of lightly salted water to a boil. Add the pasta, return to a boil, and cook for 8–10 minutes, or until tender but still firm to the bite. Add the broccoli to the saucepan for the last 4 minutes of the cooking time.

2 Meanwhile, lightly poach the salmon fillet in a saucepan of gently simmering water for 4–5 minutes (if in one piece), or until just cooked but still moist. Alternatively, cut into 2–3 even pieces and cook in a microwave oven on Medium for 2 minutes, then turn the pieces around so that the cooked parts are in the center, and cook for an additional 1 minute, or until just cooked but still moist. Using a fork, flake the flesh into a bowl.

3 Put the yogurt, milk, cheese, mustard, and pepper to taste in a separate bowl and beat together.

4 When the pasta and broccoli are cooked, drain and toss with the salmon flakes and the cheese sauce. Transfer to a warmed serving dish, garnish with parsley, and serve.

fettuccine alla bucaniera

serves 6

- 1 tbsp all-purpose flour
- 1 lb/450 g lemon sole fillets, skinned and cut into chunks
- 1 lb/450 g monkfish fillets, skinned and cut into chunks
- 6 tbsp butter
- 4 shallots, finely chopped
- 2 garlic cloves, crushed
- 1 carrot, diced
- 1 leek, finely chopped
- 1¼ cups fish stock
- 1¼ cups dry white wine
- 2 tsp Asian fish sauce
- 1 tbsp balsamic vinegar
- 1 lb/450 g dried fettuccine (thick pasta strands)
- salt and pepper
- chopped fresh flat-leaf parsley, to garnish

1 Season the flour with salt and pepper and spread out on a plate. Coat all the fish pieces with it, shaking off the excess. Melt the butter in a saucepan, add the fish, shallots, garlic, carrot, and leek, then cook over low heat, stirring frequently, for 10 minutes. Sprinkle in the remaining seasoned flour and cook, stirring constantly, for 1 minute.

2 Mix the fish stock, wine, Asian fish sauce, and balsamic vinegar together in a pitcher and gradually stir into the fish mixture. Bring to a boil, stirring constantly, then reduce the heat and simmer gently for 15 minutes.

3 Meanwhile, bring a large saucepan of lightly salted water to a boil. Add the pasta, return to a boil, and cook for 8–10 minutes, or until tender but still firm to the bite. Drain and transfer to a warmed serving dish. Spoon the fish mixture onto the pasta, garnish with chopped parsley, and serve.

italian fish stew

serves 4

- 2 tbsp olive oil
- 2 red onions, finely chopped
- 1 garlic clove, crushed
- 2 zucchini, sliced
- 14 oz/400 g canned chopped tomatoes
- 3¾ cups fish or vegetable stock
- 3 oz/85 g dried conchiglie (pasta shells)
- 12 oz/350 g firm white fish, such as cod, haddock, or hake, skinned, boned, and cut into chunks
- 1 tbsp chopped fresh basil or oregano, plus extra to garnish
- 1 tsp grated lemon rind
- 1 tbsp cornstarch
- 1 tbsp water
- salt and pepper

1 Heat the oil in a large saucepan. Add the onions and garlic and cook over low heat, stirring occasionally, for about 5 minutes, until softened. Add the zucchini and cook, stirring frequently, for 2–3 minutes.

2 Add the tomatoes and stock to the saucepan and bring to a boil. Add the pasta, bring back to a boil, reduce the heat, and cover. Simmer for 5 minutes.

3 Add the fish to the saucepan with the basil and lemon rind and simmer gently for 5 minutes, until the fish is opaque and flakes easily (be careful to avoid overcooking it) and the pasta is tender, but still firm to the bite.

4 Blend the cornstarch with the water to a smooth paste and stir into the stew. Cook gently for 2 minutes, stirring constantly, until thickened. Season to taste with salt and pepper.

5 Ladle the stew into a warmed serving dish. Garnish with basil and serve immediately.

tagliatelle with creamy shrimp

serves 4

- 3 tbsp olive oil
- 3 tbsp butter
- 4 garlic cloves, finely chopped
- 2 tbsp finely diced red bell pepper
- 2 tbsp tomato paste
- ½ cup dry white wine
- 1 lb/450 g dried tagliatelle (thick pasta strands)
- 12 oz/350 g shrimp, peeled, cut into ½-inch/1-cm pieces
- ½ cup heavy cream
- salt and pepper
- chopped fresh flat-leaf parsley, to garnish

1 Heat the oil and butter in a pan over medium–low heat. Add the garlic and red bell pepper. Cook for a few seconds, or until the garlic is just beginning to color. Stir in the tomato paste and wine. Cook for 10 minutes, stirring.

2 Meawhile, bring a large saucepan of lightly salted water to a boil. Add the pasta, return to a boil, and cook for 8–10 minutes, or until tender but still firm to the bite. Drain and keep warm.

3 Add the shrimp to the sauce and raise the heat to medium–high. Cook for 2 minutes, stirring, until the shrimp turn pink. Reduce the heat and stir in the cream. Cook for 1 minute, stirring constantly, until thickened. Season to taste with salt and pepper.

4 Transfer the pasta to a warmed serving dish. Pour the sauce over the pasta. Sprinkle with the parsley. Toss well to mix and serve.

fusilli with shrimp & peas

serves 4

- pinch of saffron threads
- 1 cup dry white wine
- 3 tbsp olive oil
- 2 tbsp unsalted butter
- 1 shallot, chopped
- 2 cups peas
- 12 oz/350 g cooked peeled shrimp
- 12 oz/350 g dried fusilli (pasta spirals)
- salt and pepper
- chopped fresh dill, to garnish

1 Place the saffron in a small bowl, add the wine, and let soak. Heat the olive oil and butter in a large heavy-bottom skillet. Add the shallot and cook over low heat, stirring occasionally, for 5 minutes, or until softened. Add the peas and shrimp and cook, stirring occasionally, for 2–3 minutes.

2 Bring a large saucepan of lightly salted water to a boil. Add the pasta, return to a boil, and cook for 8–10 minutes, or until tender but still firm to the bite.

3 Meanwhile, stir the saffron-and-wine mixture into the skillet. Increase the heat and cook until the liquid is reduced by about half. Season to taste with salt and pepper. Drain the pasta and add to the skillet. Cook for 1–2 minutes, or until it is well coated with the sauce. Transfer to a warmed serving dish, sprinkle with dill, and serve.

tagliatelle with shrimp & scallops

serves 6

- 1 lb/450 g shrimp
- 2 tbsp butter
- 2 shallots, finely chopped
- 1 cup dry white vermouth
- 1½ cups water
- 1 lb/450 g dried linguine (thin pasta strands)
- 2 tbsp olive oil
- 1 lb/450 g prepared scallops
- 2 tbsp chopped fresh chives
- salt and pepper

1 Shell and devein the shrimp, reserving the shells. Melt the butter in a heavy-bottom skillet. Add the shallots and cook over low heat, stirring occasionally, for 5 minutes, or until softened. Add the shrimp shells and cook, stirring constantly, for 1 minute. Pour in the vermouth and cook, stirring, for 1 minute. Add the water, bring to a boil, then reduce the heat and let simmer for 10 minutes, or until the liquid has reduced by half. Remove the skillet from the heat.

2 Bring a large saucepan of lightly salted water to a boil. Add the pasta, return to a boil, and cook for 8–10 minutes, or until tender but still firm to the bite.

3 Meanwhile, heat the oil in a separate heavy-bottom skillet. Add the scallops and shrimp and cook, stirring frequently, for 2 minutes, or until the scallops are opaque and the shrimp have changed color. Strain the shrimp-shell stock into the skillet. Drain the pasta and add to the skillet with the chives and season to taste with salt and pepper. Toss well over a low heat for 1 minute, transfer to a warmed serving dish, and serve.

linguine with clams

serves 2–4

- 7 oz/200 g dried linguine (thin pasta strands)
- 3 tbsp extra virgin olive oil
- 4 garlic cloves, finely chopped
- 2 shallots, finely chopped
- ½ fresh red chile, finely chopped
- ½ cup white wine
- 2 lb 4 oz/1 kg fresh clams, cleaned
- handful fresh flat-leaf parsley, chopped
- zest of 1 lemon
- salt and pepper

1 Bring a large saucepan of lightly salted water to a boil. Add the pasta, return to a boil, and cook for 8–10 minutes, or until tender but still firm to the bite.

2 Meanwhile, add half the olive oil to a large saucepan with a lid and place over high heat. Add the garlic, shallots, and chile and cook gently for 8–10 minutes, until softened. Add the wine, bring to a boil, and cook for 2 minutes. Add the clams, cover, and cook for an additional 2–5 minutes, or until all the clams have opened. Discard any clams that remain closed. Add the drained linguine, parsley, lemon zest, the remaining olive oil, and some salt and pepper and mix through.

3 Transfer to a warmed serving dish and serve with another bowl for discarded shells.

spaghetti with crab

serves 4

- 1 dressed crab, about 1 lb/450 g including the shell
- 12 oz/350 g dried spaghetti
- 6 tbsp extra virgin olive oil
- 1 fresh red chile, seeded and finely chopped
- 2 garlic cloves, finely chopped
- 3 tbsp chopped fresh parsley
- 2 tbsp lemon juice
- 1 tsp finely grated lemon rind
- salt and pepper
- lemon wedges, to garnish

1 Using a knife, scoop the meat from the crab shell into a bowl. Mix the white and brown meat lightly together and set aside.

2 Bring a large saucepan of lightly salted water to a boil over medium heat. Add the pasta, return to a boil, and cook for 8–10 minutes, or until tender but still firm to the bite. Drain thoroughly and return to the pan.

3 Meanwhile, heat 2 tablespoons of the oil in a skillet over low heat. Add the chile and garlic and cook for 30 seconds, then add the crabmeat, parsley, lemon juice, and lemon rind. Cook for an additional minute, or until the crabmeat is just heated through.

4 Add the crab mixture to the pasta with the remaining oil and season to taste with salt and pepper. Toss together thoroughly, then transfer to a large, warmed serving dish. Garnish with a few lemon wedges and serve.

conchiglie with mussels

serves 6

- 2 lb 12 oz/1.25 kg mussels, scrubbed and debearded
- 1 cup dry white wine
- 2 large onions, chopped
- ½ cup butter
- 6 large garlic cloves, finely chopped
- 5 tbsp chopped fresh parsley
- 1¼ cups heavy cream
- 14 oz/400 g dried conchiglie (pasta shells)
- salt and pepper

1 Discard any mussels with broken shells or any that refuse to close when tapped. Place the mussels in a large, heavy-bottom pan, together with the wine and half of the onions. Cover and cook over medium heat, shaking the pan frequently, for 2–3 minutes, or until the shells open. Remove the pan from the heat. Strain the mussels and reserve the cooking liquid. Discard any mussels that remain closed. Strain the cooking liquid through a cheesecloth-lined strainer into a bowl and set aside.

2 Melt the butter in a pan. Add the remaining onion and cook until translucent. Stir in the garlic and cook for 1 minute. Gradually stir in the reserved cooking liquid. Stir in the parsley and cream, and season to taste. Simmer over a low heat.

3 Bring a large saucepan of lightly salted water to a boil. Add the pasta, return to a boil, and cook for 8–10 minutes, or until tender but still firm to the bite. Drain and keep warm.

4 Set aside a few mussels for garnish and remove the remainder from their shells. Stir the shelled mussels into the sauce and warm briefly. Transfer the pasta to a warmed serving dish. Pour over the sauce and toss to coat. Garnish with the reserved mussels and serve.

penne with squid & tomatoes

serves 4

- 8 oz/225 g dried penne (pasta quills)
- 12 oz/350 g prepared squid
- 6 tbsp olive oil
- 2 onions, sliced
- 1 cup fish or chicken stock
- ⅔ cup full-bodied red wine
- 14 oz/400 g canned chopped tomatoes
- 2 tbsp tomato paste
- 1 tbsp chopped fresh marjoram
- 1 bay leaf
- salt and pepper
- chopped fresh flat-leaf parsley, to garnish

1 Bring a large saucepan of lightly salted water to a boil. Add the pasta, return to a boil, and cook for 3 minutes, then drain and set aside until ready to use. With a sharp knife, cut the squid into strips.

2 Heat the olive oil in a large saucepan. Add the onions and cook over low heat, stirring occasionally, for 5 minutes, or until softened. Add the squid and stock, bring to a boil, and simmer for 3 minutes. Stir in the wine, chopped tomatoes and their can juices, tomato paste, marjoram, and bay leaf. Season to taste with salt and pepper. Bring to a boil and cook for 5 minutes, or until slightly reduced.

3 Add the pasta, return to a boil, and simmer for 5–7 minutes, or until tender but still firm to the bite. Remove and discard the bay leaf. Transfer to a warmed serving dish, sprinkle with the parsley, and serve.

baked scallops with pasta in shells

serves 4

- 12 scallops
- 2 tbsp olive oil
- 12 oz/350 g dried conchiglie (pasta shells)
- scant ⅔ cup fish stock
- 1 onion, chopped
- juice and finely grated rind of 2 lemons
- ½ cup heavy cream
- 2 cups grated cheddar cheese
- salt and pepper

1 Preheat the oven to 350°F/180°C. Remove the scallops from their shells. Scrape off the skirt and the black intestinal thread. Reserve the white part (the flesh) and the orange part (the coral or roe). Carefully ease the flesh and coral from the shell with a short but strong knife. Wash and dry the shells. Put the shells on a cookie sheet. Sprinkle lightly with the oil and set aside.

2 Meanwhile, bring a large saucepan of lightly salted water to a boil. Add the pasta, return to a boil, and cook for 8–10 minutes, or until tender but still firm to the bite. Drain and divide the pasta among the scallop shells.

3 Put the scallops, stock, and onion in an ovenproof dish and season to taste. Cover with foil and bake in the oven for 8 minutes.

4 Remove the dish from the oven. Remove the foil and transfer the scallops to the shells. Add 1 tablespoon of the cooking liquid to each shell, together with a drizzle of lemon juice, a little lemon rind, and cream, then top with the grated cheese.

5 Increase the oven temperature to 450°F/230°C and return the scallops to the oven for an additional 4 minutes. Transfer to a warmed serving dish, add extra seasoning if liked, and serve.

Mmmm... vegetarian

pasta with pesto

serves 4

- 1 lb/450 g dried tagliatelle (thick pasta strands)
- fresh basil sprigs, to garnish

pesto

- 2 garlic cloves
- ¼ cup pine nuts
- large pinch of salt
- 2½ cups fresh basil leaves
- ½ cup freshly grated Parmesan cheese
- ½ cup olive oil

1 To make the pesto, put the garlic, pine nuts, salt, and the basil into a mortar, and pound to a paste with a pestle. Transfer to a bowl and gradually work in the Parmesan cheese with a wooden spoon, followed by the olive oil, to make a thick, creamy sauce. Taste and adjust the seasoning if necessary.

2 Alternatively, put the garlic, pine nuts, and salt into a food processor or blender and process briefly. Add the basil leaves and process to a paste. With the motor still running, gradually add the olive oil. Scrape into a bowl and beat in the Parmesan. Season to taste with salt.

3 Bring a large saucepan of lightly salted water to a boil. Add the pasta, return to a boil, and cook for 8–10 minutes, or until tender but still firm to the bite. Drain the pasta well, return to the saucepan, and toss with half the pesto, then transfer to a warmed serving dish and top with the remaining pesto. Garnish with basil sprigs and serve immediately.

pasta all'arrabbiata

serves 4

- ⅔ cup dry white wine
- 1 tbsp sun-dried tomato paste
- 2 fresh red chiles
- 2 garlic cloves, finely chopped
- 12 oz/350 g dried tortiglioni (pasta tubes)
- 4 tbsp chopped fresh flat-leaf parsley
- fresh Romano cheese shavings, to serve
- salt and pepper

sugocasa

- 5 tbsp extra virgin olive oil
- 1 lb/450 g plum tomatoes, chopped

1 To make the sugocasa, heat the oil in a skillet over a high heat until almost smoking. Add the tomatoes and cook, stirring frequently, for 2–3 minutes. Reduce the heat to low and cook gently for 20 minutes, or until soft. Season to taste with salt and pepper. Press through a nonmetallic strainer with a wooden spoon into a saucepan.

2 Add the wine, tomato paste, whole chiles, and garlic to the sugocasa, and bring to a boil. Reduce the heat and simmer gently.

3 Meanwhile, bring a large saucepan of lightly salted water to a boil. Add the pasta, return to a boil, and cook for 8–10 minutes, or until tender but still firm to the bite.

4 Remove the chiles and taste the sauce. If you prefer a hotter flavor, chop some or all of the chiles and return to the pan. Check and adjust the seasoning, if necessary, then stir in half the parsley.

5 Drain the pasta and transfer to a warmed serving dish. Add the sauce and toss to coat. Sprinkle with the remaining parsley and serve with the cheese shavings.

penne primavera

serves 4

- 1 cup baby corn
- ½ cup whole baby carrots
- 1¼ cups shelled fava beans
- generous 1 cup whole green beans, cut into 1-inch/2.5-cm pieces
- 12 oz/350 g dried penne (pasta quills)
- 1¼ cups low-fat plain yogurt
- 1 tbsp chopped fresh parsley
- 1 tbsp chopped fresh chives
- salt and pepper
- fresh chives, to garnish

1 Bring a large saucepan of slightly salted water to a boil. Add the corn and carrots and cook for 5 minutes, or until tender. Remove the vegetables with a slotted spoon, drain, and rinse under cold running water.

2 Return the vegetable cooking water to a boil, add the fava beans and green beans, and cook for 3–4 minutes, until tender, then drain and rinse under cold running water. Slip the skins off the fava beans.

3 Bring a large saucepan of lightly salted water to a boil. Add the pasta, return to a boil, and cook for 8–10 minutes, or until tender but still firm to the bite. Meanwhile, put the yogurt, parsley, chopped chives, and salt and pepper in a bowl and mix together.

4 Drain the pasta and return to the pan. Add the vegetables and yogurt sauce, heat gently, and toss together, until hot.

5 Transfer to a warmed serving dish, garnish with chives, add extra seasoning, if liked, and serve.

pappardelle with pumpkin sauce

serves 4

- 4 tbsp butter
- 6 shallots, finely chopped
- 1 lb 12 oz/800 g pumpkin, peeled, seeded, and cut into pieces
- pinch of freshly grated nutmeg
- ¾ cup light cream
- 4 tbsp freshly grated Parmesan cheese, plus extra to serve
- 2 tbsp chopped fresh flat-leaf parsley
- 12 oz/350 g dried pappardelle (thick pasta strands)
- salt

1 Melt the butter in a large, heavy-bottom pan. Add the shallots, sprinkle with a little salt, cover, and cook over low heat, stirring occasionally, for 30 minutes.

2 Add the pumpkin pieces and season with nutmeg to taste. Cover and cook over low heat, stirring occasionally, for 40 minutes, or until the pumpkin is pulpy. Stir in the cream, Parmesan, and parsley, and remove the pan from the heat.

3 Meanwhile, bring a large saucepan of lightly salted water to a boil. Add the pasta, return to a boil, and cook for 8–10 minutes, or until tender but still firm to the bite. Drain, reserving 2–3 tablespoons of the cooking water.

4 Add the pasta to the pumpkin mixture and stir in the reserved cooking water if the mixture seems too thick. Cook, stirring constantly, for 1 minute, then transfer to a warmed serving dish and serve immediately with extra grated Parmesan.

fusilli with zucchini & lemon

serves 4

- 6 tbsp olive oil
- 1 small onion, thinly sliced
- 2 garlic cloves, finely chopped
- 2 tbsp chopped fresh rosemary
- 1 tbsp chopped fresh flat-leaf parsley
- 1 lb/450 g small zucchini, cut into 1½-inch/4-cm strips
- finely grated rind of 1 lemon
- 1 lb/450 g dried fusilli (pasta spirals)
- salt and pepper
- freshly grated Parmesan cheese, to serve

1 Heat the oil in a large skillet over low–medium heat. Add the onion and cook gently, stirring occasionally, for about 10 minutes, until golden.

2 Increase the heat to medium–high. Add the garlic, rosemary, and parsley. Cook for a few seconds, stirring.

3 Add the zucchini and lemon rind. Cook for 5–7 minutes, stirring occasionally, until just tender. Season to taste with salt and pepper. Remove from the heat.

4 Bring a large saucepan of lightly salted water to a boil. Add the pasta, return to a boil, and cook for 8–10 minutes, or until tender but still firm to the bite. Drain the pasta and transfer to a warmed serving dish.

5 Briefly reheat the zucchini sauce. Pour over the pasta and toss well to mix. Transfer to a warmed serving dish and serve with the Parmesan.

chile broccoli pasta

serves 4

- 8 oz/225 g dried penne (pasta quills)
- 3 cups small broccoli florets
- ¼ cup extra virgin olive oil
- 2 large garlic cloves, chopped
- 2 fresh red chiles, seeded and diced
- 8 cherry tomatoes
- salt
- small handful of fresh basil, to garnish

1 Bring a large saucepan of lightly salted water to a boil. Add the pasta, return to a boil, and cook for 8–10 minutes, or until tender but still firm to the bite. Drain.

2 Bring a saucepan of lightly salted water to a boil, add the broccoli, and cook for 5 minutes. Drain, rinse with cold water, and drain again.

3 Heat the olive oil in the saucepan that the pasta was cooked in. Add the garlic, chiles, and tomatoes. Cook over high heat for 1 minute.

4 Return the broccoli to the saucepan with the tomato mixture and mix well. Cook for 2 minutes to heat through. Add the pasta and mix well again. Cook for an additional minute.

5 Remove the pasta from the heat, turn into a warmed serving dish, and serve garnished with basil.

garlic spaghetti

serves 4

- ½ cup olive oil
- 3 garlic cloves, crushed
- pinch of salt
- 1 lb/450 g dried spaghetti
- 3 tbsp coarsely chopped fresh flat-leaf parsley
- pepper

1 Heat the oil in a saucepan. Add the garlic and salt and cook over low heat, stirring constantly, until golden brown, then remove the saucepan from the heat.

2 Bring a large saucepan of lightly salted water to a boil. Add the pasta, return to a boil, and cook for 8–10 minutes, or until tender but still firm to the bite. Drain and return to the saucepan.

3 Add the olive oil-and-garlic mixture to the pasta and toss to coat thoroughly. Season to taste with pepper, then add the chopped fresh parsley and toss to coat again.

4 Transfer the pasta to a warmed serving dish and serve.

rigatoni with bell peppers & goat cheese

serves 4

- 2 tbsp olive oil
- 1 tbsp butter
- 1 small onion, finely chopped
- 4 bell peppers, yellow and red, seeded and cut into ¾-inch/2-cm squares
- 3 garlic cloves, thinly sliced
- 1 lb/450 g dried rigatoni (pasta tubes)
- 4½ oz/125 g goat cheese, crumbled
- 15 fresh basil leaves, shredded
- 10 black olives, pitted and sliced
- salt and pepper

1 Heat the oil and butter in a large skillet over medium heat. Add the onion and cook until soft. Raise the heat to medium–high and add the bell peppers and garlic. Cook for 12–15 minutes, stirring, until the peppers are tender but not mushy. Season to taste with salt and pepper. Remove from the heat.

2 Bring a large saucepan of lightly salted water to a boil. Add the pasta, return to a boil, and cook for 8–10 minutes, or until tender but still firm to the bite. Drain and transfer to a warmed serving dish. Add the goat cheese and toss to mix.

3 Briefly reheat the onion-and-pepper mixture. Add the basil and olives. Pour over the pasta and toss well to mix. Transfer to a warmed serving dish and serve.

pasta shapes with pumpkin sauce

serves 4

- 4 tbsp butter
- ⅔ cup finely chopped white onion or shallots
- 1 lb 12 oz/800 g pumpkin
- pinch of freshly grated nutmeg
- 12 oz/350 g dried penne or radiatore (large pasta shapes)
- generous ¾ cup light cream
- 4 tbsp freshly grated Parmesan cheese, plus extra to serve
- 2 tbsp chopped fresh flat-leaf parsley
- salt and pepper

1 Melt the butter in a saucepan over low heat. Add the onions, sprinkle with a little salt, cover, and cook, stirring frequently, for 25–30 minutes.

2 Scoop out and discard the seeds from the pumpkin. Peel and finely chop the flesh. Tip the pumpkin into the saucepan and season to taste with nutmeg. Cover and cook over low heat, stirring occasionally, for 45 minutes.

3 Meanwhile, bring a large saucepan of lightly salted water to a boil. Add the pasta, return to a boil, and cook for 8–10 minutes, or until tender but still firm to the bite. Drain thoroughly, reserving about ⅔ cup of the cooking liquid.

4 Stir the cream, grated Parmesan, and parsley into the pumpkin sauce and season to taste with salt and pepper. If the mixture seems a little too thick, add some or all of the reserved cooking liquid and stir. Add the pasta and toss for 1 minute. Transfer to a warmed serving dish and serve with extra grated Parmesan.

fusilli with ricotta, mint & garlic

serves 4

- 10½ oz/300 g dried fusilli (pasta spirals)
- ½ cup ricotta cheese
- 1–2 roasted garlic cloves from a jar, finely chopped
- ⅔ cup heavy cream
- 1 tbsp chopped fresh mint, plus extra sprigs to garnish
- salt and pepper

1 Bring a large saucepan of lightly salted water to a boil. Add the pasta, return to a boil, and cook for 8–10 minutes, or until tender but still firm to the bite.

2 Beat the ricotta, garlic, cream, and chopped mint together in a bowl until smooth.

3 Drain the cooked pasta, then add back into the pan. Pour in the cheese mixture and toss together.

4 Transfer to a warmed serving dish and season with pepper. Garnish with the mint sprigs and serve.

spaghetti with fava beans

serves 4

- 1⅔ cups shelled fava beans
- 1 lb 2 oz/500 g dried spaghetti
- salt and pepper

pea pesto

- 3 cups fresh shelled peas
- 5 tbsp extra virgin olive oil
- 2 garlic cloves, crushed
- scant 1 cup freshly grated Parmesan cheese, plus extra, shaved, for serving
- ⅔ cup blanched almonds, chopped
- pinch of sugar

1 To make the pesto, bring a saucepan of lightly salted water to a boil, add the peas, and cook for 2–3 minutes, or until just tender. Drain and transfer to a blender or food processor. Add the oil, garlic, and cheese and process to a coarse paste. Add the almonds and process again. Add the sugar and season to taste with salt and pepper. Set aside.

2 Blanch the fava beans in a saucepan of salted boiling water until just tender. Drain and let cool. Peel off the dull skins.

3 Bring a large saucepan of lightly salted water to a boil. Add the pasta, return to a boil, and cook for 8–10 minutes, or until tender but still firm to the bite. Drain, then stir in the fava beans and toss with the pesto. Transfer to a warmed serving dish, season with pepper, and serve with the shaved Parmesan.

penne with mixed beans

serves 4

- 1 tbsp olive oil
- 1 onion, chopped
- 1 garlic clove, finely chopped
- 1 carrot, finely chopped
- 1 celery stalk, finely chopped
- 15 oz/425 g canned mixed beans, drained and rinsed
- 1 cup strained tomatoes
- 1 tbsp chopped fresh chervil, plus extra leaves to garnish
- 12 oz/350 g dried penne (pasta quills)
- salt and pepper

1 Heat the olive oil in a large, heavy-bottom skillet. Add the onion, garlic, carrot, and celery, and cook over low heat, stirring occasionally, for 5 minutes, or until the onion has softened.

2 Add the mixed beans, strained tomatoes, and chopped chervil to the skillet and season with salt and pepper to taste. Cover and simmer gently for 15 minutes.

3 Meanwhile, bring a large saucepan of lightly salted water to a boil. Add the pasta, return to a boil, and cook for 8–10 minutes, or until tender but still firm to the bite. Drain the pasta and transfer to a warmed serving dish. Add the mixed bean sauce, toss well, and serve immediately, garnished with extra chervil.

creamy spinach & mushroom pasta

serves 4

- 10½ oz/300 g dried penne (pasta quills)
- 2 tbsp olive oil
- 9 oz/250 g white mushrooms, sliced
- 1 tsp dried oregano
- scant 1¼ cups vegetable stock
- 1 tbsp lemon juice
- 6 tbsp cream cheese
- 1 cup frozen spinach leaves
- salt and pepper

1 Bring a large saucepan of lightly salted water to a boil. Add the pasta, return to a boil, and cook for 8–10 minutes, or until tender but still firm to the bite. Drain, reserving ¾ cup of the cooking liquid.

2 Meanwhile, heat the oil in a large, heavy-bottom skillet over medium heat, add the mushrooms, and cook, stirring frequently, for 8 minutes, or until almost crisp. Stir in the oregano, stock, and lemon juice and cook for 10–12 minutes, or until the sauce is reduced by half.

3 Stir in the cream cheese and spinach and cook over medium–low heat for 3–5 minutes. Add the reserved cooking liquid, then the cooked pasta. Stir well, season to taste with salt and pepper, and heat through. Transfer to a warmed serving dish and serve.

pasta with olive sauce

serves 2–4

- 12 oz/350 g dried pasta shapes
- 6 tbsp olive oil
- ½ tsp freshly grated nutmeg
- ½ tsp pepper
- 1 garlic clove, crushed
- 2 tbsp tapenade
- ½ cup black or green olives, pitted and sliced
- chopped fresh flat-leaf parsley, to garnish
- salt

1 Bring a large saucepan of lightly salted water to a boil. Add the pasta, return to a boil, and cook for 8–10 minutes, or until tender but still firm to the bite.

2 Meanwhile, put ½ teaspoon of salt with the oil, nutmeg, pepper, garlic, tapenade, and olives in another saucepan and heat slowly but do not allow to boil. Cover and let stand for 3–4 minutes.

3 Drain the pasta and return to the saucepan. Add the olives in the flavored oil and heat gently for 1–2 minutes. Transfer to a warmed serving dish and serve immediately garnished with chopped parsley.

spaghetti with tomatoes & basil

serves 4

- 5 tbsp extra virgin olive oil
- 1 onion, finely chopped
- 1 lb 12 oz/800 g canned chopped tomatoes
- 4 garlic cloves, cut into quarters
- 1 lb/450 g dried spaghetti
- large handful fresh basil leaves, shredded
- salt and pepper
- shavings of fresh Parmesan cheese, to serve

1 Heat the oil in a large pan over medium heat. Add the onion and cook gently for 5 minutes, until soft. Add the tomatoes and garlic. Bring to a boil, then simmer over medium–low heat for 25–30 minutes, or until the oil separates from the tomato. Season to taste with salt and pepper.

2 Bring a large saucepan of lightly salted water to a boil. Add the pasta, return to a boil, and cook for 8–10 minutes, or until tender but still firm to the bite. Drain and transfer to a warmed serving dish.

3 Pour the sauce over the pasta. Add the basil and toss well to mix. Transfer to a warmed serving dish and serve with the Parmesan.

fettuccine with tomatoes & olives

serves 4

- 4 plum tomatoes, peeled, seeded, and chopped
- 4 garlic cloves, finely chopped
- 8 black olives, pitted and finely chopped
- 1 red chile, seeded and finely chopped
- 2 tbsp chopped fresh flat-leaf parsley
- 2 tbsp extra virgin olive oil
- 1 tbsp lemon juice
- 10 oz/280 g dried fettuccine (thick pasta strands)
- salt and pepper

1 Place the tomatoes in a large, nonmetallic strainer set over a bowl. Cover and set aside in the refrigerator for 30 minutes.

2 Combine the garlic, olives, chile, parsley, oil, and lemon juice in a separate bowl. Season to taste with salt and pepper. Cover and set aside in the refrigerator until required.

3 Add the tomatoes to the garlic mixture, discarding the drained juice.

4 Bring a large saucepan of lightly salted water to a boil. Add the pasta, return to a boil, and cook for 8–10 minutes, or until tender but still firm to the bite. Drain, transfer to a warmed serving dish and add the garlic-and-tomato mixture. Toss well, add extra seasoning, if liked, and serve.

penne with asparagus & bleu cheese

serves 4

- 1 lb/450 g asparagus tips
- olive oil, for drizzling
- 8 oz/225 g bleu cheese, crumbled
- ¾ cup heavy cream
- 12 oz/350 g dried penne (pasta quills)
- salt and pepper

1 Preheat the oven to 450°F/230°C. Place the asparagus tips in a single layer in a shallow ovenproof dish. Drizzle with a little olive oil. Season to taste with salt and pepper. Turn to coat in the oil and seasoning.

2 Roast in the preheated oven for 10–12 minutes, or until slightly browned and just tender. Set aside and keep warm.

3 Combine the crumbled cheese with the cream in a bowl. Season to taste with salt and pepper.

4 Bring a large saucepan of lightly salted water to a boil. Add the pasta, return to a boil and cook for 8–10 minutes, or until tender but still firm to the bite. Drain and transfer to a warmed serving dish.

5 Add the asparagus and the cheese mixture to the pasta. Toss well until the cheese has melted and the pasta is coated with the sauce. Transfer to a warmed serving dish, add extra seasoning, if liked, and serve.

tagliatelle with wild mushrooms

serves 4

- 1 lb/450 g dried tagliatelle (thick pasta strands)
- 4 tbsp butter
- 1 garlic clove, crushed
- 8 oz/225 g mixed wild mushrooms, sliced
- generous 1 cup mascarpone cheese
- 2 tbsp milk
- 1 tsp chopped fresh sage, plus extra whole leaves to garnish
- salt and pepper
- freshly grated Parmesan cheese, to serve

1 Bring a large saucepan of lightly salted water to a boil. Add the pasta, return to a boil, and cook for 8–10 minutes, or until tender but still firm to the bite.

2 Meanwhile, melt the butter in a separate large pan. Add the garlic and mushrooms and cook for 3–4 minutes.

3 Reduce the heat and stir in the mascarpone cheese, milk, and sage. Season to taste with salt and pepper.

4 Drain the pasta thoroughly and add to the mushroom sauce. Toss until the pasta is well coated with the sauce. Transfer to a warmed serving dish, garnish with sage leaves, add extra seasoning, if liked, and serve with the Parmesan.

spaghetti alla norma

serves 4

- 3/4 cup olive oil
- 1 lb 2 oz/500 g plum tomatoes, peeled and chopped
- 1 garlic clove, chopped
- 12 oz/350 g eggplant, diced
- 14 oz/400 g dried spaghetti
- 1/2 bunch fresh basil, torn
- 1 1/3 cups freshly grated Romano cheese
- salt and pepper

1 Heat 4 tablespoons of the oil in a large pan. Add the tomatoes and garlic, season to taste with salt and pepper, cover, and cook over low heat, stirring occasionally, for 25 minutes.

2 Meanwhile, heat the remaining oil in a heavy skillet. Add the eggplant and cook, stirring occasionally, for 5 minutes, until evenly golden brown. Remove with a slotted spoon and drain on paper towels.

3 Bring a large saucepan of lightly salted water to a boil. Add the pasta, return to a boil, and cook for 8–10 minutes, until tender but still firm to the bite.

4 Meanwhile, stir the drained eggplant into the pan of tomatoes. Taste and adjust the seasoning, if necessary.

5 Drain the pasta and place in a warmed serving dish. Add the tomato-and-eggplant mixture, basil, and half the Romano cheese. Toss well, sprinkle with the remaining cheese, and serve.

pasta with green vegetables

serves 4

- 8 oz/225 g dried fusilli (pasta spirals)
- 1 head broccoli, cut into florets
- 2 zucchini, sliced
- 8 oz/225 g asparagus spears, trimmed
- 2 cups snow peas
- 1 cup frozen peas
- 2 tbsp butter
- 3 tbsp vegetable stock
- 5 tbsp heavy cream
- large pinch of freshly grated nutmeg
- 2 tbsp chopped fresh flat-leaf parsley
- salt and pepper
- freshly grated Parmesan cheese, to serve

1 Bring a large saucepan of lightly salted water to a boil. Add the pasta, return to a boil, and cook for 8–10 minutes, or until tender but still firm to the bite. Drain the pasta, return to the saucepan, cover, and keep warm.

2 Steam the broccoli, zucchini, asparagus spears, and snow peas over a pan of boiling, salted water until just starting to soften. Remove from the heat and plunge into cold water to prevent further cooking. Drain and reserve. Bring a saucepan of slightly salted water to a boil, add the peas, and cook for 3 minutes. Drain, refresh in cold water, and drain again.

3 Place the butter and vegetable stock in a pan over medium heat. Add all the vegetables, except the asparagus spears, and toss carefully with a wooden spoon to heat through, being careful not to break them up. Stir in the cream, let the sauce heat through, and season with salt, pepper, and nutmeg to taste.

4 Transfer the pasta to a warmed serving dish and stir in the chopped parsley. Spoon the sauce over the pasta and arrange the asparagus spears on top. Sprinkle with the Parmesan and serve hot.

Mmmm...
filled & baked

lasagna al forno

serves 4

- 2 tbsp olive oil
- 2 oz/55 g pancetta, chopped
- 1 onion, chopped
- 1 garlic clove, finely chopped
- 8 oz/ 225 g fresh ground beef
- 2 celery stalks, chopped
- 2 carrots, chopped
- pinch of sugar
- ½ tsp dried oregano
- 14 oz/400 g canned chopped tomatoes
- 2 tsp Dijon mustard
- 1¼ cups grated cheddar cheese
- 1¼ cups hot Béchamel Sauce (see page 10)
- 8 oz/225 g dried no-precook lasagna sheets
- 1 cup freshly grated Parmesan cheese, plus extra for sprinkling
- salt and pepper

1 Preheat the oven to 375°F/190°C. Heat the olive oil in a large saucepan. Add the pancetta and cook over medium heat, stirring occasionally, for 3 minutes, or until the fat starts to run. Add the onion and garlic and cook, stirring occasionally, for 5 minutes, or until softened.

2 Add the beef and cook, breaking it up with a wooden spoon, until browned all over. Stir in the celery and carrots and cook for 5 minutes. Season to taste with salt and pepper. Add the sugar, oregano, and tomatoes and their can juices. Bring to a boil, reduce the heat, and simmer for 30 minutes.

3 Meanwhile, to make the cheese sauce, stir the mustard and cheddar cheese into the hot Béchamel Sauce.

4 In a large, rectangular ovenproof dish, make alternate layers of meat sauce, lasagna sheets, and Parmesan. Pour the cheese sauce over the layers, covering them completely, and sprinkle with Parmesan. Bake in the preheated oven for 30 minutes, or until golden brown and bubbling. Serve.

mixed meat lasagna

serves 6

- 1 onion, chopped
- 1 carrot, chopped
- 1 celery stalk, chopped
- 3 oz/85 g pancetta, chopped
- 6 oz/175 g fresh ground beef
- 6 oz/175 g fresh ground pork
- 3 tbsp olive oil
- ⅓ cup red wine
- ⅔ cup beef stock
- 1 tbsp tomato paste
- 1 bay leaf
- 1 clove
- ⅔ cup milk
- 14 oz/400 g dried no-precook lasagna sheets
- 2½ cups Béchamel Sauce (see page 10)
- 1¼ cups freshly grated Parmesan
- 5 oz/140 g mozzarella, diced
- 4 tbsp butter, diced
- salt and pepper

1 Mix the onion, carrot, celery, pancetta, beef, and pork together in a large bowl. Heat the olive oil in a large, heavy-bottom skillet, add the meat mixture, and cook over medium heat, breaking up the meat with a wooden spoon, until it is browned all over. Pour in the wine, then bring to a boil and cook until reduced. Pour in ½ cup of the stock, bring to a boil, and cook until reduced.

2 Mix the tomato paste and remaining stock together in a small bowl, then add to the skillet with the bay leaf and clove. Season to taste with salt and pepper and pour in the milk. Cover and simmer for 1 hour.

3 Preheat the oven to 400°F/200°C. Remove and discard the bay leaf and the clove from the meat sauce. In a large ovenproof dish, make alternate layers of lasagna sheets, meat sauce, Béchamel Sauce, Parmesan, and mozzarella cheese. Finish with a layer of Béchamel Sauce and sprinkle with the remaining Parmesan.

4 Dot the top of the lasagna with butter and bake in the preheated oven for 25 minutes, or until golden brown. Serve.

chicken & spinach lasagna

serves 4

- 12 oz/350 g frozen chopped spinach, thawed and drained
- ½ tsp ground nutmeg
- 3¼ cups diced, cooked lean chicken
- 6 oz/175 g dried no-precook lasagna sheets
- 1½ tbsp cornstarch
- scant 2 cups milk
- 4 tbsp freshly grated Parmesan cheese
- salt and pepper

tomato sauce

- 14 oz/400 g canned chopped tomatoes
- 1 medium onion, finely chopped
- 1 garlic clove, crushed
- ⅔ cup white wine
- 3 tbsp tomato paste
- 1 tsp dried oregano

1 Preheat the oven to 400°F/200°C. To make the tomato sauce, place the tomatoes in a pan and stir in the onion, garlic, wine, tomato paste, and oregano. Bring to a boil and simmer for 20 minutes, until thick. Season to taste with salt and pepper.

2 Drain the spinach again and pat dry on paper towels. Arrange the spinach in the bottom of an ovenproof dish. Sprinkle with nutmeg and season to taste.

3 Arrange the diced chicken over the spinach and spoon the tomato sauce over it. Arrange the sheets of lasagna over the tomato sauce.

4 Blend the cornstarch with a little of the milk to make a paste. Pour the remaining milk into a pan and stir in the cornstarch paste. Heat gently for 2–3 minutes, stirring constantly, until the sauce thickens. Season to taste with salt and pepper.

5 Spoon the sauce over the lasagna to cover it completely and transfer the dish to a cookie sheet. Sprinkle the Parmesan over the sauce and bake in the preheated oven for 25 minutes, until golden brown and bubbling. Serve.

lasagna alla marinara

serves 6

- 1 tbsp butter
- 8 oz/225 g shrimp, shelled, deveined, and coarsely chopped
- 1 lb/450 g monkfish fillets, skinned and chopped
- 8 oz/225 g cremini mushrooms, chopped
- 3½ cups Béchamel Sauce (see page 10)
- 14 oz/400 g canned chopped tomatoes
- 1 tbsp chopped fresh chervil
- 1 tbsp shredded fresh basil
- 6 oz/175 g dried no-precook lasagna sheets
- ¾ cup freshly grated Parmesan cheese
- salt and pepper

1 Preheat the oven to 375°F/190°C. Melt the butter in a large saucepan. Add the shrimp and monkfish and cook over medium heat for 3–5 minutes, or until the shrimp change color. Using a slotted spoon, transfer the shrimp to a small heatproof bowl. Add the mushrooms to the pan and cook, stirring occasionally, for 5 minutes. Transfer the fish and mushrooms to the bowl.

2 Stir the fish mixture, with any juices, into the Béchamel Sauce and season to taste with salt and pepper. Layer the tomatoes, chervil, basil, fish mixture, and lasagna sheets in a large ovenproof dish, ending with a layer of the fish mixture. Sprinkle evenly with the grated Parmesan.

3 Bake in the preheated oven for 35 minutes, or until golden brown. Serve.

vegetable lasagna

serves 4

- olive oil, for brushing
- 2 eggplants, sliced
- 2 tbsp butter
- 1 garlic clove, finely chopped
- 4 zucchini, sliced
- 1 tbsp finely chopped fresh flat-leaf parsley
- 1 tbsp finely chopped fresh marjoram
- 8 oz/225 g mozzarella cheese, grated
- 2½ cups strained tomatoes
- 6 oz/175 g dried no-precook lasagna sheets
- 2½ cups Béchamel Sauce (see page 10)
- ½ cup freshly grated Parmesan cheese
- salt and pepper

1 Preheat the oven to 400°F/200°C. Brush a large ovenproof dish with olive oil. Brush a large grill pan with olive oil and heat until smoking. Add half the eggplants and cook over medium heat for 8 minutes, or until golden brown all over. Remove from the grill pan and drain on paper towels. Add the remaining eggplant slices and extra oil, if necessary, and cook for 8 minutes, or until golden brown all over.

2 Melt the butter in a skillet and add the garlic, zucchini, parsley, and marjoram. Cook over medium heat for 5 minutes, or until the zucchini are golden brown. Remove from the skillet and let drain on paper towels.

3 Layer the eggplants, zucchini, grated mozzarella, strained tomatoes, and lasagna sheets in the dish, seasoning with salt and pepper as you layer and finish with a layer of lasagna. Pour over the Béchamel Sauce, making sure that all the pasta is covered. Sprinkle with the Parmesan and bake in the preheated oven for 30–40 minutes, or until golden brown. Serve.

spinach & mushroom lasagna

serves 4

- ½ cup butter, plus extra for greasing
- 2 garlic cloves, finely chopped
- 4 oz/115 g shallots
- 8 oz/225 g wild mushrooms
- 1 cup spinach, cooked, drained, and chopped finely
- 2⅔ cups freshly grated cheddar cheese
- ¼ tsp freshly grated nutmeg
- 1 tsp chopped fresh basil
- 4 tbsp all-purpose flour
- 2½ cups hot milk
- 6 oz/175 g dried no-precook lasagna sheets
- salt and pepper

1 Preheat the oven to 400°F/200°C. Lightly grease an ovenproof dish with a little butter.

2 Melt 4 tablespoons of the butter in a pan over low heat. Add the garlic, shallots, and wild mushrooms and cook for 3 minutes. Stir in the spinach, 2 cups of the cheddar cheese, the nutmeg, and basil. Season to taste with salt and pepper, then set aside.

3 Melt the remaining butter in another pan over low heat. Add the flour and cook, stirring constantly, for 1 minute. Gradually stir in the hot milk, whisking constantly, until smooth. Stir in ¼ cup of the remaining cheese and season to taste with salt and pepper.

4 Spread half the mushroom mixture over the bottom of the prepared dish. Cover with a layer of lasagna sheets, then with half the cheese sauce. Repeat the process and sprinkle over the remaining cheese. Cook in the preheated oven for 30 minutes, or until golden brown. Serve.

double cheese macaroni

serves 4

- 8 oz/225 g dried macaroni
- generous 1 cup ricotta cheese
- 1½ tbsp whole-grain mustard
- 3 tbsp snipped fresh chives, plus extra to garnish
- 1⅓ cups halved cherry tomatoes
- scant 1 cup chopped, drained sun-dried tomatoes in oil
- butter, for greasing
- scant 1 cup grated cheddar cheese
- salt and pepper

1 Bring a large saucepan of lightly salted water to a boil. Add the pasta, return to a boil, and cook for 8–10 minutes, or until tender but still firm to the bite. Drain.

2 Preheat the broiler. Mix together the ricotta, mustard, and chives with salt and pepper to taste. Stir in the macaroni, cherry tomatoes, and sun-dried tomatoes.

3 Grease a 7½-cup shallow ovenproof dish. Spoon in the macaroni into the prepared dish, spreading evenly.

4 Sprinkle the cheddar cheese over the macaroni mixture and cook under the preheated broiler for 4–5 minutes, until golden and bubbling. Serve.

beef & macaroni bake

serves 4

- 2 tbsp olive oil
- 1 large onion, chopped
- 8 oz/225 g fresh ground beef
- 1 garlic clove, finely chopped
- 14 oz/400 g canned chopped tomatoes
- 1 tbsp tomato paste
- 6 oz/175 g dried macaroni
- butter, for greasing
- 3 eggs, separated
- ½ cup freshly grated Parmesan cheese, plus extra to serve
- salt and pepper

1 Preheat the oven to 375°F/190°C. Heat the olive oil in a large, heavy-bottom skillet. Add the onion and cook over low heat, stirring occasionally, for 5 minutes, or until softened. Add the beef and cook, breaking up the meat with a wooden spoon, until browned. Stir in the garlic, tomatoes and their can juices, and tomato paste, then season to taste with salt and pepper. Bring to a boil, reduce the heat, and simmer for 20 minutes, then remove the skillet from the heat and let cool slightly.

2 Meanwhile, bring a large saucepan of lightly salted water to a boil. Add the pasta, return to a boil, and cook for 8–10 minutes, or until tender but still firm to the bite. Drain and set aside.

3 Lightly grease a 5-cup soufflé dish. Beat the egg yolks and add them to the meat sauce, then stir in the pasta. Whisk the egg whites until stiff peaks form, then fold into the sauce. Spoon the mixture into the prepared dish, sprinkle with the grated Parmesan, and bake in the preheated oven for 45 minutes, or until well risen and golden brown. Sprinkle with extra Parmesan and serve.

macaroni & tuna casserole

serves 2

- 5 oz/140 g dried macaroni
- 1 tbsp olive oil
- 1 garlic clove, crushed
- 1 cup sliced white mushrooms
- ½ red bell pepper, thinly sliced
- 7 oz/200 g canned tuna in spring water, drained and flaked
- ½ tsp dried oregano
- 2 tbsp butter or margarine, plus extra for greasing
- 1 tbsp all-purpose flour
- 1 cup milk
- 2 tomatoes, sliced
- 2 tbsp dried breadcrumbs
- ½ cup grated sharp cheddar or Parmesan cheese
- salt and pepper

1 Preheat the oven to 400°F/200°C. Bring a large saucepan of lightly salted water to a boil. Add the pasta, return to a boil, and cook for 8–10 minutes, or until tender but still firm to the bite. Drain, rinse, and drain thoroughly.

2 Heat the olive oil in a skillet and cook the garlic, mushrooms, and bell pepper until soft. Add the tuna and oregano, and season to taste with salt and pepper. Heat through.

3 Grease a 4-cup/1-liter ovenproof dish with a little butter. Add half of the cooked macaroni to the prepared dish, cover with the tuna mixture, then add the remaining macaroni.

4 Melt the butter in a pan, stir in the flour, and cook for 1 minute. Add the milk gradually and bring to a boil. Simmer for 1–2 minutes, stirring constantly, until thickened. Season to taste with salt and pepper. Pour the sauce over the macaroni. Lay the sliced tomatoes over the sauce and sprinkle with the breadcrumbs and cheese. Cook in the preheated oven for 25 minutes, or until piping hot and the top is well browned. Serve.

hot tomato & conchiglie gratin

serves 4

- 1 onion, chopped
- 14 oz/400 g canned chopped tomatoes
- 1 cup milk
- 1–2 red chiles, seeded and finely chopped
- 1 garlic clove, finely chopped
- pinch of ground coriander
- 10 oz/280 g dried conchiglie (pasta shells)
- ¾ cup grated Gruyère cheese
- salt and pepper

1 Preheat the broiler. Put the onion, tomatoes, and milk in a large saucepan and bring just to a boil. Add the chiles, garlic, coriander, and pasta, season to taste with salt and pepper, and cook over medium heat, stirring frequently, for 2–3 minutes.

2 Add just enough water to cover and cook, stirring frequently, for 8–10 minutes, or until the pasta is tender but still firm to the bite.

3 Spoon the pasta mixture into individual flameproof dishes and sprinkle evenly with the cheese. Place under the preheated broiler for 3–4 minutes, until the cheese has melted. Serve.

cannelloni with ham & ricotta

serves 4

- 2 tbsp olive oil
- 2 onions, chopped
- 2 garlic cloves, finely chopped
- 1 tbsp shredded fresh basil
- 1 lb 12 oz/800 g canned chopped tomatoes
- 1 tbsp tomato paste
- 10–12 dried cannelloni tubes
- butter, for greasing
- 1 cup ricotta cheese
- ¾ cup diced, cooked ham
- 1 egg
- ½ cup freshly grated Romano cheese
- salt and pepper

1 Preheat the oven to 350°F/180°C. Heat the olive oil in a large, heavy-bottom skillet. Add the onions and garlic and cook over low heat, stirring occasionally, for 5 minutes, or until the onion is softened. Add the basil, chopped tomatoes and their can juices, and tomato paste, and season to taste with salt and pepper. Reduce the heat and simmer for 30 minutes, or until thickened.

2 Meanwhile, bring a large saucepan of lightly salted water to a boil. Add the pasta, return to a boil, and cook for 8–10 minutes, or until tender but still firm to the bite. Using a slotted spoon, transfer the cannelloni tubes to a large plate and pat dry with paper towels.

3 Grease a large, shallow ovenproof dish with butter. Mix the ricotta, ham, and egg together in a bowl and season to taste with salt and pepper. Using a teaspoon, fill the cannelloni tubes with the ricotta mixture and place in a single layer in the prepared dish. Pour the tomato sauce over the cannelloni and sprinkle with the grated Romano cheese. Bake in the preheated oven for 30 minutes, or until golden brown. Serve.

chicken & mushroom cannelloni

serves 4

- butter, for greasing
- 2 tbsp olive oil
- 2 garlic cloves, crushed
- 1 large onion, finely chopped
- 8 oz/225 g wild mushrooms, sliced
- 12 oz/350 g fresh ground chicken
- 4 oz/115 g prosciutto, diced
- ⅔ cup Marsala wine
- 7 oz/200 g canned chopped tomatoes
- 1 tbsp shredded fresh basil leaves
- 2 tbsp tomato paste
- 10–12 dried cannelloni tubes
- 2½ cups Béchamel Sauce (see page 10)
- ¾ cup freshly grated Parmesan cheese
- salt and pepper
- chopped fresh flat-leaf parsley, to garnish

1 Preheat the oven to 375°F/190°C. Lightly grease a large ovenproof dish. Heat the olive oil in a heavy-bottom skillet. Add the garlic, onion, and mushrooms, and cook over low heat, stirring frequently, for 8–10 minutes. Add the ground chicken and prosciutto and cook, stirring frequently, for 12 minutes, or until browned all over. Stir in the Marsala, tomatoes and their can juices, basil, and tomato paste, and cook for 4 minutes. Season to taste with salt and pepper, then cover and simmer for 30 minutes. Uncover, stir, and simmer for 15 minutes.

2 Meanwhile, bring a large saucepan of lightly salted water to a boil. Add the pasta, return to a boil, and cook for 8–10 minutes, or until tender but still firm to the bite. Using a slotted spoon, transfer the cannelloni tubes to a plate and pat dry with paper towels.

3 Using a teaspoon, fill the cannelloni tubes with the chicken-and-mushroom mixture. Transfer them to the dish. Pour the Béchamel Sauce over them to cover completely and sprinkle with the grated Parmesan.

4 Bake in the preheated oven for 30 minutes, or until golden brown and bubbling. Serve, garnished with the parsley.

mushroom cannelloni

serves 4

- 12 dried cannelloni tubes
- 6 tbsp olive oil, plus extra for brushing
- 1 onion, finely chopped
- 2 garlic cloves, finely chopped
- 1 lb 12 oz/800 g canned chopped tomatoes
- 1 tbsp tomato paste
- 8 black olives, pitted and chopped
- 2 tbsp butter
- 1 lb/450 g wild mushrooms, finely chopped
- 1½ cups fresh breadcrumbs
- ⅔ cup milk
- 1 cup ricotta cheese
- 6 tbsp freshly grated Parmesan cheese
- 2 tbsp pine nuts
- 2 tbsp slivered almonds
- salt and pepper

1 Preheat the oven to 375°F/190°C. Bring a large saucepan of lightly salted water to a boil. Add the pasta, return to a boil, and cook for 8–10 minutes, or until tender but still firm to the bite. Transfer the cannelloni tubes to a plate and pat dry. Brush a large ovenproof dish with olive oil.

2 Heat 2 tablespoons of the oil in a skillet, add the onion and half the garlic and cook over low heat for 5 minutes, or until softened. Add the tomatoes and their can juices, tomato paste, and olives, and season to taste with salt and pepper. Bring to a boil and cook for 3–4 minutes. Pour the sauce into the ovenproof dish.

3 To make the filling, melt the butter in a heavy-bottom skillet. Add the mushrooms and remaining garlic and cook over medium heat, stirring frequently, for 3–5 minutes, or until tender. Remove the skillet from the heat. Mix the breadcrumbs, milk, and remaining oil together in a large bowl, then stir in the ricotta, mushroom mixture, and 4 tablespoons of the Parmesan cheese. Fill the cannelloni tubes with the mushroom mixture and place them in the dish. Brush with olive oil and sprinkle with the remaining Parmesan, the pine nuts, and almonds. Bake in the oven for 25 minutes, or until golden. Serve.

sicilian linguine

serves 4

- ½ cup olive oil
- 2 eggplants, sliced
- 12 oz/350 g fresh ground beef
- 1 onion, chopped
- 2 garlic cloves, finely chopped
- 2 tbsp tomato paste
- 14 oz/400 g canned chopped tomatoes
- 1 tsp Worcestershire sauce
- 1 tbsp chopped fresh flat-leaf parsley
- ⅓ cup pitted black olives, sliced
- 1 red bell pepper, seeded and chopped
- 6 oz/175 g dried linguine (thin pasta strands)
- 1 cup freshly grated Parmesan cheese
- salt and pepper

1 Preheat the oven to 400°F/200°C. Brush an 8-inch/20-cm springform, round cake pan with oil and line the bottom with parchment paper. Heat half the oil in a skillet. Add the eggplants in batches, and cook until lightly browned on both sides. Add more oil as needed. Drain the eggplants on paper towels, then arrange in overlapping slices to cover the bottom and sides of the cake pan, reserving a few slices.

2 Heat the remaining olive oil in a large pan and add the beef, onion, and garlic. Cook over medium heat, breaking up the meat with a wooden spoon, until browned all over. Add the tomato paste, tomatoes and their can juices, Worcestershire sauce, and parsley. Season to taste with salt and pepper and simmer for 10 minutes. Add the olives and bell pepper and cook for 10 minutes.

3 Meanwhile, bring a saucepan of lightly salted water to a boil. Add the pasta, return to a boil, and cook for 8–10 minutes, or until tender but still firm to the bite. Drain and transfer to a bowl. Add the meat sauce and Parmesan and toss, then spoon into the cake pan, press down, and cover with the remaining eggplant slices. Bake in the preheated oven for 40 minutes. Let stand for 5 minutes, then loosen around the edges and invert onto a plate. Remove and discard the parchment paper and serve.

stuffed eggplants

serves 4

- 3 tbsp olive oil, for brushing
- 8 oz/225 g dried penne (pasta quills)
- 2 eggplants
- 1 large onion, chopped
- 2 garlic cloves, crushed
- 14 oz/400 g canned chopped tomatoes
- 2 tsp dried oregano
- 2 oz/55 g mozzarella cheese, thinly sliced
- ⅓ cup freshly grated Parmesan cheese
- 5 tbsp dry breadcrumbs
- salt and pepper

1 Preheat the oven to 400°F/200°C. Brush a baking sheet with oil. Bring a large saucepan of lightly salted water to a boil. Add the pasta, return to a boil, and cook for 8–10 minutes, or until tender but still firm to the bite. Drain, return to the saucepan, cover, and keep warm.

2 Cut the eggplants in half lengthwise and score around the insides with a sharp knife, being careful not to pierce the shells. Scoop out the flesh with a spoon. Brush the insides of the shells with olive oil. Chop the flesh and set aside.

3 Heat the oil in a skillet. Cook the onion over low heat for 5 minutes, until softened. Add the garlic and cook for 1 minute. Add the chopped eggplant and cook, stirring frequently, for 5 minutes. Add the tomatoes and oregano and season to taste. Bring to a boil and simmer for 10 minutes, until thickened. Remove the skillet from the heat and stir in the pasta.

4 Brush a baking sheet with oil and arrange the eggplant shells in a single layer. Divide half of the tomato-and-pasta mixture among them. Sprinkle over the slices of mozzarella, then pile the remaining tomato-and-pasta mixture on top. Mix the Parmesan and breadcrumbs and sprinkle over the top, patting lightly into the mixture.

5 Bake in the preheated oven for 25 minutes, or until the topping is golden brown. Serve.

mixed vegetable agnolotti

serves 4

- butter, for greasing
- 1 quantity Basic Pasta Dough (see page 10)
- all-purpose flour, for dusting
- ¾ cup freshly grated Parmesan
- salt and pepper

filling

- ½ cup olive oil
- 1 red onion, chopped
- 3 garlic cloves, chopped
- 2 large eggplants, cut into chunks
- 3 large zucchini, cut into chunks
- 6 beefsteak tomatoes, peeled, seeded, and coarsely chopped
- 1 large green bell pepper, seeded and diced
- 1 large red bell pepper, seeded and diced
- 1 tbsp sun-dried tomato paste
- 1 tbsp shredded fresh basil

1 To make the filling, heat the olive oil in a large, heavy-bottom pan. Add the onion and garlic and cook over low heat, stirring occasionally, for 5 minutes, or until softened. Add the eggplants, zucchini, tomatoes, green and red bell peppers, sun-dried tomato paste, and basil. Season to taste with salt and pepper, cover, and simmer gently, stirring occasionally, for 20 minutes.

2 Lightly grease an ovenproof dish with butter. Roll out the pasta dough on a lightly floured surface and stamp out 3-inch/7.5-cm circles with a fluted pastry cutter. Place a spoonful of the vegetable filling on each circle. Dampen the edges slightly and fold the pasta circles over, pressing together to seal. Place on a floured dish towel and let stand for 1 hour. Preheat the oven to 400°F/200°C.

3 Bring a large saucepan of lightly salted water to a boil. Add the pasta, in batches if necessary, return to a boil, and cook for 8–10 minutes, or until tender but still firm to the bite. Remove with a slotted spoon, drain, and transfer to the dish. Sprinkle with the Parmesan and bake in the preheated oven for 20 minutes. Serve.

chicken tortellini

serves 4

- 4 oz/115 g skinless, boneless chicken breast
- 2 oz/55 g prosciutto
- 1½ oz/40 g cooked spinach, well drained
- 1 tbsp finely chopped onion
- 6 tbsp freshly grated Parmesan cheese
- pinch of ground allspice
- 2 eggs, beaten
- 2 quantities Basic Pasta Dough (see page 10)
- all-purpose flour, for dusting
- salt and pepper
- chopped fresh flat-leaf parsley, to garnish
- salt and pepper

sauce

- 1¼ cups light cream
- 2 garlic cloves, crushed
- 1 cup thinly sliced button mushrooms

1 Bring a saucepan of salted water to a boil. Add the chicken and poach for about 10 minutes. Let cool slightly, then place in a food processor with the prosciutto, spinach, and onion and process until finely chopped. Stir in 2 tablespoons of the Parmesan, the allspice, and half the eggs and season with salt and pepper.

2 Roll out the pasta dough on a lightly floured counter to a rectangle 1/16–1/8 inch/2–3 mm thick. Using a 2-inch/5-cm plain cookie cutter, stamp out circles. Place about 1 teaspoon of the filling in the center of each circle. Brush the edges with a little beaten egg, then fold in half to make a half moon, pressing the edges to seal. Wrap the half moon around the tip of your index finger until the corners meet and press to seal. Repeat with the remaining pasta half moons. Place the filled tortellini on a floured dish towel and let stand for 1 hour.

3 Bring a large saucepan of lightly salted water to a boil. Add the pasta, in batches if necessary, return to a boil, and cook for 8–10 minutes, or until tender but still firm to the bite. Drain on kitchen paper and transfer to a serving dish.

4 To make the sauce, bring the cream and garlic to a boil in a small saucepan, then simmer for 3 minutes. Add the mushrooms and 2 tablespoons of the Parmesan, season, and simmer for 2–3 minutes. Pour the sauce over the tortellini. Sprinkle over the remaining Parmesan and garnish with the parsley.

beef ravioli

serves 6

- 3 tbsp olive oil
- 5 tbsp butter
- 12 oz/350 g braising beef, in a single piece
- 1 red onion, finely chopped
- 1 celery stalk, finely chopped
- 1 carrot, finely chopped
- ⅔ cup red wine
- 1 cup beef stock
- 1 tbsp tomato paste
- 1 cup fresh breadcrumbs
- 4 tbsp freshly grated Parmesan cheese
- pinch of freshly grated nutmeg
- pinch of ground cinnamon
- 2 eggs, lightly beaten
- 1½ quantities Basic Pasta Dough (see page 10)
- all-purpose flour, for dusting
- salt and pepper

1 Heat the oil and half the butter in a large pan. Add the beef and cook over medium heat for 8–10 minutes. Remove the beef from the pan. Lower the heat and add the onion, celery, and carrot to the pan. Cook for 5 minutes, until softened. Return the beef to the pan, add the wine, and cook until reduced by two-thirds.Combine the stock and tomato paste, stir into the pan, and season. Cover and simmer gently, for 3 hours, until the meat is tender. Remove the beef and let cool.

2 Mix the breadcrumbs and half the Parmesan in a bowl and stir in about half of the sauce (discard the remaining sauce). Finely chop the beef and stir it into the breadcrumb mixture. Season and stir in the nutmeg, cinnamon, and eggs.

3 Roll out the pasta dough on a lightly floured surface to 1/16–1/8 inch/2–3 mm thick. Using a fluted 2-inch/5-cm cookie cutter, stamp out circles. Place about 1 teaspoon of the beef mixture in the center of each circle, brush the edges with water, and fold in half, pressing to seal. Place on a floured dish towel and let stand for 30 minutes. Bring a large saucepan of lightly salted water to a boil. Add the pasta, in batches if necessary, return to a boil, and cook for 8–10 minutes, or until tender but still firm to the bite.

4 Meanwhile, melt the remaining butter. Drain the ravioli and transfer to a warmed serving dish. Pour over the melted butter, sprinkle with the remaining Parmesan, and serve.

vegetable ravioli

serves 4

- 2 large eggplants
- 3 large zucchini
- 6 large tomatoes
- 1 large green bell pepper
- 1 large red bell pepper
- 3 garlic cloves
- 1 large onion
- ½ cup olive oil
- 2 tbsp tomato paste
- ½ tsp chopped fresh basil, plus extra sprigs to garnish
- 1 quantity Basic Pasta Dough (see page 10)
- all-purpose flour, for dusting
- 6 tbsp butter, for greasing
- ⅔ cup light cream
- ¾ cup freshly grated Parmesan cheese
- salt and pepper

1 To make the filling, cut the eggplants and zucchini into 1-inch/2.5-cm chunks. Put the eggplant pieces into a strainer, sprinkle liberally with salt, and set aside for 20 minutes. Rinse and drain, then pat dry on paper towels.

2 Blanch the tomatoes in boiling water for 2 minutes. Drain, peel, and chop the flesh. Core and seed the bell peppers and cut into 1-inch/2.5-cm dice. Chop the garlic and onion.

3 Heat the oil in a pan over low heat. Add the garlic and onion and cook for about 3 minutes. Stir in the eggplants, zucchini, tomatoes, bell peppers, tomato paste, and basil. Season to taste with salt and pepper, cover, and simmer for 20 minutes. Roll out the pasta dough on a lightly floured surface to a rectangle 1/16–⅛ inch/2–3 mm thick. Using a 2-inch/5-cm plain cookie cutter, stamp out circles. Place small mounds, about 1 teaspoon each, of the filling on half of the circles. Brush the edges with a little water, then cover with the remaining circles, pressing the edges to seal. Place on a floured dish towel and let stand for 1 hour. Preheat the oven to 400°F/200°C.

4 Bring a large saucepan of lightly salted water to a boil. Add the pasta, in batches if necessary, return to a boil, and cook for 8–10 minutes, or until tender but still firm to the bite. Drain and transfer to an ovenproof dish, dotting each layer with butter. Pour over the cream and sprinkle over the Parmesan. Cook in the preheated oven for 20 minutes. Garnish with basil and serve.

spinach & ricotta ravioli

serves 4

- 12 oz/350 g fresh spinach leaves, coarse stalks removed
- 1 cup ricotta cheese
- ½ cup freshly grated Parmesan cheese, plus extra to serve
- 2 eggs
- pinch of freshly grated nutmeg
- 1 quantity Spinach Pasta Dough (see pages 11)
- all-purpose flour, for dusting
- salt and pepper

1 Wash the spinach and place in a large saucepan, then cover and cook over a low heat for 5 minutes, until wilted. Drain well and squeeze out as much moisture as possible. Let cool, then chop finely. Beat the ricotta until smooth, then stir in the spinach, Parmesan, and 1 of the eggs, and season with nutmeg and pepper.

2 Divide the pasta in half and wrap 1 piece in plastic wrap. Roll out the other piece on a lightly floured surface to a rectangle 1⁄16–⅛ inch/2–3 mm thick. Cover with a damp dish towel and roll out the other piece of dough to the same size. Place small mounds, about 1 teaspoon each, of the filling in rows 1½ inches/4 cm apart on a sheet of pasta dough. In a small bowl, lightly beat the remaining egg and use it to brush the spaces between the mounds. Lift the second sheet of dough on top of the first and press down firmly between the pockets of filling. Using a pasta wheel or sharp knife. Cut into squares. Place on a floured dish towel and let stand for 1 hour.

3 Bring a large saucepan of lightly salted water to a boil. Add the pasta, in batches if necessary, return to a boil, and cook for 8–10 minutes, or until tender but still firm to the bite. Remove with a slotted spoon and drain on paper towels. Transfer to a warmed serving dish and sprinkle with Parmesan.

Index

mmm...

Mmmm...

Mmmm

Mmmm...

Mmmm...

Mmmm

n...

Mmmm..

mmm...

Mm